DELIVERING
ON
DEBT RELIEF

From IMF Gold to a
New Aid Architecture

DELIVERING
ON
DEBT RELIEF
From IMF Gold to a
New Aid Architecture

Nancy Birdsall
John Williamson
with Brian Deese

Center for Global Development
Institute for International Economics
Washington, DC
April 2002

Nancy Birdsall is president of the Center for Global Development. She was formerly with the Carnegie Endowment for International Peace and director of the Economic Reform Project there. She was the executive vice president of the Inter-American Development Bank (1993-98) and before that director of the Policy Research Department at the World Bank. She is the author of numerous publications on labor markets, human resources, economic inequality, the relationship between income distribution and growth, and other development issues. She serves on various boards, including the Population Council, and is special adviser to the administrator of the United Nations Development Program.

John Williamson, senior fellow at the Institute for International Economics since 1981, was on leave as chief economist for South Asia at the World Bank during 1996-99. He was a professor of economics at Pontifica Universidade Católica do Rio de Janeiro (1978-81), University of Warwick (1970-77), Massachusetts Institute of Technology (1967, 1980), University of York (1963-68), and Princeton University (1962-63); adviser to the International Monetary Fund (1972-74); and economic consultant to the UK Treasury (1968-70). He is author or editor of numerous studies on international monetary and developing world debt issues, including *Exchange Rate Regimes for Emerging Markets: Reviving the Intermediate Option* (2000), *The Crawling Band as an Exchange Rate Regime* (1996), and *What Role for Currency Boards?* (1995).

Brian Deese is a research assistant at the Center for Global Development. He was previously a junior fellow at the Carnegie Endowment for International Peace.

CENTER FOR GLOBAL DEVELOPMENT
1750 Massachusetts Avenue, NW
Washington, DC 20036
(202) 454-1305 FAX: (202) 454-1534
http://www.cgdev.org

Nancy Birdsall, *President*

INSTITUTE FOR INTERNATIONAL ECONOMICS
1750 Massachusetts Avenue, NW
Washington, DC 20036-1903
(202) 328-9000 FAX: (202) 328-5432
http://www.iie.com

C. Fred Bergsten, *Director*
Brigitte Coulton, *Director of Publications and Web Development*
Brett Kitchen, *Director of Marketing*

Typesetting and printing:
Automated Graphic Systems, Inc.

Printed in the United States of America
04 03 02   5 4 3 2 1

Library of Congress Cataloging-in-Publication Data

Birdsall, Nancy.
  Delivering on debt relief : from IMF gold to a new aid architecture / Nancy Birdsall, John Williamson with Brian Deese.
    p. cm.
  Includes bibliographical references and index.
  ISBN 0-88132-331-4
  1. Debt relief—Developing countries.
  2. Debts, External—Developing countries.
  3. Loans, Foreign—Developing countries.
  4. Structural adjustment (Economic policy)—Developing countries.
  I. Williamson, John, 1937- II. Deese, Brian. III. Title.

HG3891.5 .B57 2002
336.3'6—dc21   2002017283

Contents

Figures

Boxes

Foreword

In this monograph, two respected development economists collaborate to produce a current, complete, and objective assessment of the global debt issue and its effects on the poorest countries. The study examines how the poorest countries (now called HIPCs, i.e. *heavily indebted poor countries*) became so hopelessly indebted and what the richer countries (specifically the G-8, the World Bank, and the IMF) can and should do about it.

The frightening impact of the September 2001 terrorist attacks on the United States has made it clear that the developed countries run a terrible risk when they allow millions around the globe to languish in abject and hopeless poverty from which they see no escape. But, beyond the self-interest born of our concern to attack the root cause of the terrorists' zealotry, the richer countries have a moral imperative to address the issues of disease, ignorance, and poverty, which overwhelm such a significant portion of humanity.

Nowhere has this responsibility been more dramatically and effectively recognized than in the Jubilee 2000 debt relief campaign of the late 1990s. The Jubilee movement brought the issue of global debt into focus for the developed world. In the process, its objectives were advanced by political leaders as diverse in their views as Senators Tom Daschle and Jesse Helms, by religious leaders such as His Holiness the Pope, Pat Robertson, the World Jewish Relief organization, the Southern Baptist Convention, and hundreds of thousands of ordinary citizens throughout Europe and United States. The campaign culminated with the passage of significant debt relief legislation in the US Congress signed into law by President Bill Clinton.

Perhaps no single person did more to advance public and political awareness of the debt issue than the rock star, Bono, lead singer of the group known as U2. For millions, Bono has come to symbolize a new sense of global social responsibility which the debt question has sparked in the development world. Commentary by Bill Gates and Bono at the recent "Davos in New York" conference highlighted again the broad appeal and politically appealing character of the global debt question.

The author of this foreword somehow missed the Jubilee 2000 train. While the Jubilee campaign was at its zenith, I was preoccupied with advancing the success of BEA, a fast-growing software firm of which I was a cofounder. However, while channel surfing the satellite TV one evening in November of 2000, I stumbled across a film documentary polemic on the Ford Foundation-funded World Link channel called "Deadly Embrace." The film asserts that the World Bank and the IMF were culpable for the problems of debt management in the poorest countries, and that the debt and other policies of these institutions have had an extraordinary negative impact on the welfare and economic growth of the poor countries.

My wife then discovered on the web the Jubilee movement. Several months of further research and dialog with many experts brought me to the door of Fred Bergsten, Director of the Institute for International Economics, in Washington, DC. The Institute is one of the most respected and effective policy think tanks in the country. Fred and I agreed that we should jointly sponsor this monograph on the status of the debt issue today.

Our initial agreement to collaborate blossomed into a more ambitious initiative with the involvement of Nancy Birdsall, one of the coauthors of this monograph. By November, Fred, Nancy, and I had agreed to create a new policy research center to be allied with the Institute for International Economics called the *Center for Global Development.* Launched in November of 2001, the Center is now actively engaged in a wide range of development research studies under the leadership of Nancy, its President.

A key question in framing the approach to the monograph was whether shining the dispassionate light of independent academic enquiry on the debt question would result in conclusions and recommendations that would be consistent with or contrary to the views of the Jubilee debt campaigns. The enquiry reflected in this monograph has led the researchers to the position that more debt relief for the world's poorest countries would be a good thing. What a nice thing it is to have the conclusions of both hearts and minds intersect so fortuitously.

Edward W. Scott, Jr.
Cofounder
Center for Global Development

Preface

This is the first major publication of the new Center for Global Development, created in late 2001 as the only research institution in the United States specifically devoted to advancing development prospects in the world's poor countries. Fittingly, the study was conducted jointly with the Institute for International Economics, which has played a central role in the startup of, and will maintain close ties with, the new Center.

The study addresses one of the central development and poverty issues of our time: debt relief for heavily indebted poor countries (HIPCs). It is the issue that motivated the Founding Chairman of the Center, Edward W. Scott, Jr., to take the initiative that led to its creation, as described in his adjoining foreword. It is an issue to which political leaders, ordinary citizens, and such global celebrities as Bono of U2 have rallied dramatically in the last few years.

The study has three goals. First, it attempts to put in context the official debt relief programs of the last two decades, including their failure to put the poorest countries on a sustainable growth path. Second, it asks whether additional debt relief for the poorer countries would be desirable—including by comparison with alternative measures to address their development problems. Third, in an effort to be pragmatic on the policy front, it outlines several creative new ways in which additional debt relief could be financed.

The study makes several striking recommendations. It finds that more debt relief would be desirable even if it failed to provide additional resources for the poorer countries. It suggests a new benchmark for determining when a country's debt profile is "sustainable," based not on the traditional export measure but on the basic needs of people and on the logic of enhancing, not undermining, the fundamental tax and expenditure mandates of the state. It argues for augmenting the current debt relief program by insuring poor countries against drought, floods and other weather shocks, and against export price shocks that are not under its control. That insurance would transfer the real cost of unexpected shocks (and possibly overoptimistic projections of poor countries' future export income and borrowing needs), from the indebted countries to the creditors. It proposes that several countries with large populations—including Indonesia, Nigeria, and Pakistan—be added to the eligibility list for debt relief. It suggests that some of the increased cost of greater debt reduction be funded through mobilization of part or all of the remaining gold stock of the International Monetary Fund. It imbeds its debt relief proposals in a "new aid architecture," described briefly in the study and to be elaborated in subsequent publications of the Center for Global Development.

The authors of this study sought input and advice from many readers in the course of its preparation. They are particularly grateful to members of the debt relief advocacy community for their incisive and insistent (!) comments, including especially Gerry Flood, Tom Hart, and Ann Pettifor; staff members of the World Bank and IMF, especially Masood Ahmed, Ishac Diwan, and Axel van Trosenburg; staff members of the US Treasury, including Steven Radelet and William Schuerch; colleagues in the research and academic communities—Colin Bradford, William Easterly, Dani Rodrik, David Roodman, Melissa Thomas, and Nicolas van de Walle; and to such seasoned experts in international finance as Richard Cooper, Stanley Fischer, Timothy Geithner, and Edwin Truman. They also thank Michael Kremer and Ann Pettifor for their participation in a related CGD seminar on debt and aid; and other colleagues at the Carnegie Endowment for International Peace, the Center for Global Development, and the Institute for International Economics who participated in seminars at those institutions.

Finally, they wish to thank Josh Catlin and Maria Unterrainer for their research help, Rochelle Howard of the Institute for International Economics for her help with several seminars, and colleagues Andrew Stober, Brigitte Coulton, Madona Devasahayam, Marla Banov, and Katie Sweetman for production support.

Nancy Birdsall and John Williamson are thoroughly beholden to Brian Deese, who began as a research assistant and deservedly ended up as a third author, for his original contributions, his dedication to getting the data right, and his general intelligence on the complex issues. They are also immensely grateful to Fred Bergsten for his inspired suggestion to Ed Scott to do this study, his insight on commenting on our drafts, and his acuity in helping us think through our bottom line. Finally, and most importantly, we are enormously grateful to Ed, for his generous direct financial support for this work and even more for his wise combination of passion on the debt and aid issues and studied disinterest in influencing our recommendations.

The Center for Global Development is a nonprofit, nonpartisan institution dedicated to reducing global poverty and inequality through policy-oriented research and active engagement on development issues with the policy community and the public. A principal focus of the Center's work is policies of the United States and other industrialized countries that affect development prospects in poor countries, and of the international institutions such as the World Bank and the IMF that are so central to the world's development architecture.

The Center's Board of Directors includes distinguished leaders of nongovernmental organizations, former officials, business executives, and some of the world's leading scholars of development. The Center also receives advice from an Advisory Committee that comprises respected development specialists and activists. The Board of Directors bears overall responsibility for the Center's programs. The Center's President works with the Board, the Advisory Committee, and its own senior staff in setting research and program priorities, and approves all formal publications. The Center is supported by an initial significant financial contribution from Edward W. Scott, Jr., and by funding from philanthropic foundations and other organizations.

The Institute for International Economics is a private nonprofit institution for the study and discussion of international economic policy. Its purpose is to analyze important issues in that area and to develop and communicate practical new approaches for dealing with them. The Institute is completely nonpartisan.

The Institute is funded largely by philanthropic foundations. Major institutional grants are now being received from the William M. Keck, Jr. Foundation and the Starr Foundation. A number of other foundations and private corporations contribute to the highly diversified financial resources of the Institute. About 31 percent of the Institute's resources in our latest fiscal year were provided by contributors outside the United States, including about 18 percent from Japan.

The Board of Directors bears overall responsibilities for the Institute and gives general guidance and approval to its research program, including the identification of topics that are likely to become important over the medium run (one to three years), and which should be addressed by the Institute. The Director, working closely with the staff and outside Advisory Committee, is responsible for the development of particular projects and makes the final decision to publish an individual study.

The Center and the Institute hope that their studies and other activities will contribute to building a stronger foundation for international economic policy around the world. We invite readers of these publications to let us know how they think we can best accomplish this objective.

C. Fred Bergsten	Nancy Birdsall
Director	President
Institute for International Economics	Center for Global Development

1

Introduction

Jubilee 2000 was by far the most successful industrial-country movement aimed at combating world poverty for many years, perhaps in all recorded history. It succeeded not just in changing official policy, but in arousing a measure of concern among the world's rich about the state of the world's poor that had been conspicuously lacking for many years.

Jubilee promised to wind itself up at the end of 2000, but in the event it reconstituted itself (temporarily) as Drop the Debt and (more permanently) as Jubilee Plus. The decision to reincarnate appears to have been driven by two considerations. One was a belief that Jubilee's objectives had not been adequately realized, because many low-income countries still had what was judged to be an excessive debt burden, despite what is called the enhanced HIPC Initiative ("HIPC" stands for heavily indebted poor country or countries; see box 1.1). The other was a realization that the movement had achieved such political momentum that it would be a mistake to waste its potential to secure further gains.

Group A versus Group B

Both the authors of this study have devoted much of their professional careers to efforts to promote development. We therefore unreservedly welcome Jubilee's success in mobilizing concern for the cause of combating poverty. At the same time, we come from the universe of what Ravi Kanbur (2001) has characterized as Group A ("finance ministry types"), as opposed to the Group B ("civil society types") that drove Jubilee and Drop the Debt and are now driving Jubilee Plus.

1

Box 1.1 The enhanced HIPC Initiative

HIPC is an ugly acronym that stands for heavily indebted poor country (or countries). The enhanced HIPC Initiative is the latest international effort to provide debt
relief to the group of 42 countries (at last count) known as HIPCs, 34 of them in
Africa. It was first agreed on at the Group of Seven summit in Cologne in 1999,
and then formally endorsed by the IMF and World Bank at their annual meetings
in September that year.

Countries seeking to participate in the HIPC Initiative submit Poverty Reduction
Strategy Papers drawn up on the basis of consultation with civil society representatives that describe their proposed economic and social policies and programs to
reduce the poverty of their citizens, including how they propose to spend money
that they no longer have to devote to debt service. When such a paper has been
approved by the boards of the World Bank and IMF, the country in question is
entitled to debt relief of at least 90 percent from official bilateral creditors as well
as relief from the multilateral creditors meant to reduce its debt stock to what is
supposed to be a sustainable level.

Although individuals from both groups may be equally concerned
about poverty, they bring different perspectives to policy debates. This
study was motivated by a conviction that the debate on debt relief needs
a fresh look, one in which Group A analysis of the risks and trade-
offs of any particular solution are more explicitly linked to our common
objectives—which, it must be said, have been more passionately proclaimed, and with notably greater political effect, by Group B.

Thinking about HIPC has led us to many of the questions that are
commonly asked about the debt of poor countries. Appendix 1.1 summarizes our answers to ten of these questions.

In particular, our analysis highlights two shortcomings of the current
HIPC debt program. First, though more ambitious than past programs
in promising more and faster debt relief for more countries, it is not
grounded analytically in a realistic conception of the amount of debt
reduction needed for most countries to achieve a sustainable path of
growth and poverty reduction.

Second, though the HIPC program is described as part of a new approach
to development assistance in the poorest countries, its design focuses on
improving the performance of recipient countries. It does not change the
perverse political and bureaucratic incentives that led the official donors
and creditors to provide the stream of loans that became unmanageable
debt in the first place. In our analysis and recommendations, we therefore
focus on the merits of debt reduction not only as part of a larger effort to
create the conditions for sustainable growth in recipient countries, but as
a critical first step in the building of a "new aid architecture."

To understand where to go next, one should first ask how the HIPCs
got to where they are today. We therefore give a sketch of the evolution
of the HIPC Initiative to date. We then ask whether the HIPCs and other

poor countries still need more help from the donors than they are currently getting, including what they received as a result of the enhanced HIPC Initiative. Two criteria that have been widely endorsed by the international community are used to make this evaluation. One is whether debt burdens are sustainable, which is the criterion explicitly stated to be the rationale for the enhanced HIPC Initiative. The other is whether these countries would have access to enough external resources to achieve the Millennium Development Goals, if they make maximum domestic efforts to that end. We conclude that there is indeed a compelling case for further action on the basis of those two criteria.

In our view, that conclusion does not suffice to make a case for further debt relief; it is also necessary to ask whether debt relief is the right *way* to deliver additional help, the alternative being a stepped-up foreign aid program. We use five criteria to judge the relative merits of these two approaches. The first is political resonance: whether and why debt relief has more political appeal in donor countries than foreign aid. The second is additionality: whether, given the answer to the first question, debt relief will bring extra resources to the cause of development or simply substitute for what might have been larger future aid flows.

The third criterion is redistribution: to the extent that additionality is less than 100 percent, one has to ask who will pay for debt relief and worry that debt relief for some poor countries (e.g., Nicaragua and Uganda) might come at the expense of equally poor countries whose governments avoided acquiring unsustainable debt (e.g., Bangladesh and India). The latter group might after all make better use of the resources in reducing poverty. The fourth is efficiency: whether and in what ways debt relief can lead to greater development effectiveness than an aid program of the same size and whether debt reduction in some circumstances could encourage additional private investment. The fifth is donor selectivity: whether debt relief can free donors from defensive lending driven by a desire to avoid defaults, and enable them to direct aid to those countries best able to use it to reduce poverty.

We conclude that some measure of debt reduction has certain advantages over simply increasing foreign aid by an equivalent amount. These advantages justify a greater and more predictable degree of debt reduction than currently envisioned (though not a complete write-off). In particular, debt reduction is a much more efficient form of transfer than traditional project-based foreign aid and loans in countries that can manage the resources well. It has the peculiar advantage of automatically improving donor coordination and enabling borrower ownership of reform programs, thus reducing the bureaucratic and management costs of a process that generally taxes rather than supports recipient countries' limited institutional capacity.

Moreover, debt reduction enables donors and creditors to escape their own bad (though generally well-intentioned) tendency of defensive lending to heavily indebted countries. In effect, sufficient debt reduction could put all the low-income debtor countries (some of which are not included in the current HIPC program) in a position to meet reasonable tests of performance in managing resources well. It would free creditors to be more selective with new grants and loans, channeling aid to those countries that both need additional resources and actually do perform. A clearly manageable debt might also encourage the ultimate keys to growth in these countries, namely, greater investor confidence and increased private investment. We conclude that it makes sense to provide for some additional debt reduction—enough to ensure that the remaining debt burden is predictably and visibly sustainable in all low-income countries.

Expanding Debt Relief

We therefore suggest expanded debt relief along the following lines:

- enlargement of debt reduction if debt service still exceeds 2 percent of GNP, to ensure that a country's budget is not made unmanageable by debt service;

- expansion of eligibility for the HIPC Initiative, and indeed our expanded proposals, to all low-income countries; and

- creation of a contingent facility to safeguard countries for 10 years against being pushed back into unsustainable debt levels by circumstances beyond their control.

Over and above the current estimated cost of the enhanced HIPC program of $29 billion (in net present value terms),[1] we estimate that these proposals would entail additional costs of between $30 billion and $80 billion (the latter including Indonesia) plus the cost of the contingency facility. The amount is large relative to the size of the planned reduction under the enhanced HIPC program, but it is not particularly large relative to current total estimated official development assistance (ODA) of $56 billion a year.

We set out proposals for financing this additional relief that we believe are financially reasonable and politically achievable, particularly if they manage to attract the support of Group B debt and development activists. Mobilization of IMF gold could cover the IMF's share of the cost of deepening and including additional countries in the initiative, and the

---

1. The amount of debt is often expressed in net present value terms. The NPV takes into account the fact that amounts owed in the future impose less of a burden than an equal amount owed now, for the same face value. The NPV of HIPCs' current debt is about $107 billion.

contingency facility. These costs would be about $9 billion, plus that of the contingency arrangement, which we estimate at $5 billion.

Beyond the IMF costs, our proposals imply an additional contribution by donors of between $20 and $70 billion (again depending on Indonesia) above the $29 billion that they have already pledged. Some of this cost (approximately $11 billion) has already been agreed to in principle by the bilateral donors that have pledged a 100 percent write-off of HIPC debts owed directly to them and through a Paris Club deal with Pakistan in December 2001. Furthermore, much of this "cost" in forsaken bilateral debt service payments is fictitious. The loans in question really ought to be written off, because the only way that the donors can ever expect to collect the debt service due is by continued defensive lending to give poor countries the foreign exchange to pay them. Writing off those loans does not involve increased donor outlays, if the donors decide not to replace the defensive lending. Finally, higher interest rates on multilateral bank loans to the upper-middle-income countries could complement allocation of a part of the additional aid to the World Bank's trust fund to pay for multilateral debt cancellation; that could finance an additional $4 billion in debt reduction over 10 years.

But debt reduction alone is not enough to get development in the poorest countries back on the rails. Central to our recommendations is our view that debt reduction should be only a first step in the reinvention of the development assistance process. After all, the fact is that the debt problem in the poorest countries reflects an unpleasant reality. Billions of dollars and hundreds of development loans for dozens of donor-driven programs during more than three decades have in many countries not resulted in sustainable growth and poverty reduction but in the accumulation of unmanageable debt. This is not true everywhere. Countries such as Bangladesh, India, and (at least until 1997) Indonesia made sufficiently good investments to enable them to service low-interest-rate loans without difficulty. But in a large number of the world's poorest countries, most of them now HIPCs, years of development assistance have not worked.

There are many possible explanations for the failures of development assistance. We return to these in our discussion of the critiques of the HIPC Initiative in the next chapter. Suffice it to say here that countries ran into difficulties in servicing their debts for various reasons: because some loans served to sell goods that were of little use to the recipient country; because some leaders were crooks who stole the money; because some loans were made to satisfy political and bureaucratic rather than development imperatives of donors; because some leaders were misguided and adopted unwise policies that blocked development; and because many countries suffered unfavorable shocks.

When it became difficult to service the debt, the first reaction of donors was to evergreen the loans; the second to reschedule the debts; the third to lower interest rates; the fourth to convert new loans to grants; and fifth, beginning in the late 1980s, to negotiate multiple rounds of debt rescheduling and debt-service relief. By the 1990s, the debt overhang of the poorest countries had become more and more visible and embarrassing. The donors and debtors seemed caught in burdensome rounds of negotiation, as well as pressure for new lending to finance countries' debt service.

The response of the international donor community has been to place its bets on two new steps. The first is to give countries a supposed fresh start by writing off "enough" of their debt through the HIPC Initiative. The second is a new kind of poverty-oriented conditionality meant to change the incentives faced by recipient countries. Countries are required to prepare a Poverty Reduction Strategy Paper (a PRSP; see box 1.1), through active citizen and civil society participation, demonstrating "ownership" by participant governments of adequate strategies. The PRSPs are meant to guide both debt relief under the HIPC Initiative and to trigger and guide new lending and grantmaking from the donor-creditor community.

The new approach is a step in the right direction. But it adds to the immediate administrative burden on the borrowers without acknowledging any responsibility of the official creditors for the unsustainable debt. In particular, the new approach fails to recognize more explicitly that official debt is for all practical purposes uncollectible (without imposing impossible burdens on already impoverished populations). Perhaps as a result, it does not build in mechanisms for greater future discipline on the part of official creditors. We are concerned that without broader reforms there is not likely to be any break from the past practices of poor donor coordination and lack of discipline in lending due to political and bureaucratic pressures. And without demonstrated improvement in the effectiveness of development assistance, we doubt that donor allocations for the poorest countries will rise.

Reinventing the Aid Architecture

Thus, we conclude that debt reduction should be seen as only a first step in a larger reinvention of the international aid architecture. In this book, we do not address the changes needed in the recipient countries, namely, critical reforms in their governance and institutions as well as their social and economic policies; that is more than one other study in itself. However, we do outline the essential features of an aid architecture that would create the right incentives for donors to support fully and effectively those countries that are making progress in reducing poverty and improving human development indicators, while discouraging finance to the governments of countries that are not.

Our most dramatic (though not new) recommendation is for increased reliance by bilateral donors on a multilateral approach, including subscribing to a "common pool" in which they would abandon project financing and tied aid, placing their funds in a pool that the government of a country making progress could spend as it saw fit. Our proposal also includes eliminating the PRSP as a necessary trigger for debt reduction. This, among other things, would recognize more explicitly the uncollectibility of much official debt and thus the creditors' as well as debtors' responsibility for past failures.

We also propose allowing the International Development Association (IDA) and the other concessional windows in the regional banks to make grants as well as loans, which we believe would have the advantage of increasing the pressure to be selective. Finally, we propose shifting the resources of the IMF's PRGF to the World Bank to make the Bank more singularly accountable for the effectiveness of what are now combined IMF and World Bank responsibilities and financing in the HIPCs.

As and when a new approach to dispensing aid begins to yield real benefits in terms of faster development and poverty reduction, we expect it to become easier to make the political case in donor countries for a greatly increased level of aid to the poorest countries, beyond that which we recommend for additional debt-stock reduction. That is also an essential element of a new aid architecture.

Meanwhile, increased aid can be directed to programs that are less dependent on the policies of a single recipient government, such as the fight against malaria, tuberculosis, and HIV/AIDS, as advocated by the World Health Organization's Commission on Macroeconomics and Health (WHO Commission 2001).

Appendix 1.1
Ten Questions about Debt and Debt Relief

1. How much debt is there, and to whom is it owed?
Debt owed by the HIPCs is about $170 billion (in 1999 nominal terms). Almost 50 percent of this is owed to bilateral creditors—mostly the United States, Japan, France, and other countries of Europe. Another 37 percent is owed to multilateral creditors: the World Bank, IMF, and the regional and subregional development banks; and 13 percent to private creditors (almost all of which is backed by a sovereign guarantee).

The debt of the HIPCs represents only 8 percent of the developing world's approximate $2 trillion debt, and only 35 percent of the debt of all the low-income countries (using the World Bank's country classification of low-income, which includes India, Indonesia, Nigeria, and Pakistan: See appendix B). For the developing world as a whole, about 25 percent of debt is owed to bilaterals, 17 percent to multilaterals, and the remaining 60 percent to private creditors (half of which is not covered by a sovereign guarantee). For a breakdown of the debt owed by each HIPC, see table 2.4.

2. What portion of the debt stock of the poorest countries would be deemed uncollectible and written off or canceled if conventional accounting practices of commercial banks were followed?
Commercial banks would eventually be required to provision against debt that has lost much of its value. One measure of the value of commercial debt is the price it commands in the market. In the late 1980s, $1 of commercial debt of countries like Bolivia and Nicaragua (now HIPCs) was worth as little as 10 cents on the dollar in the market. This means that the market judged about 90 percent of its value to be uncollectible.

Most HIPC debt is owed not to commercial but to official creditors, so there is no such market measure. However, the US government—which is congressionally mandated to estimate the present value of its loan portfolio and expense reductions in value as they occur—applies a 92 percent discount to the HIPC debt. Yet in 1999, HIPCs paid about 85 percent of the debt service they were due to pay—but they were only able to do this because of big receipts of new aid.

3. What portion of the debt of the poorest countries would be labeled "unjust" or "odious" by reasonable observers?
"Odious" debt has been legally defined as debt assumed by governments without the consent of the people and not for their benefit. During the past three decades, as much as 60 percent of private and public loans were committed by creditors to countries subsequently labeled as not free, or corrupt in the year of the commitment, according to some international indices. In the Democratic Republic of Congo (formerly Zaire), Nicaragua, Pakistan, and other heavily indebted poor countries, there were periods when governments borrowed heavily to purchase military equipment of

little benefit to ordinary citizens (Nicaragua in the 1970s), to invest in white elephant projects (Pakistan in the 1970s), or to pad the foreign bank accounts of corrupt dictators (Zaire under Mobutu). (See appendix C.)

One approach is to label as odious all debt assumed by "odious" governments—because even borrowing for good projects by odious governments may have simply made it easier to steal or misuse domestic resources. A simple measure of odious or unjust debt might then be all debt assumed by such governments. Unfortunately, labeling and quantifying odious debt does not provide much useful guidance on how much to forgive now—as we explain in the text.

4. Who should be asked to pay for debt relief?

In a conventional bankruptcy proceeding, the creditors are expected to recognize that their assets are worth less than face value, and have them scaled down to what the debtor can afford to pay. Almost all of the debt of the poorest countries is owed to official, not private commercial creditors. That means that it has been rich-country governments that have either loaned directly to poor-country governments, or have allowed the World Bank, IMF, or other institutions that they control to make the now "bad" loans. So when push comes to shove, the taxpayers of rich countries are the creditors of poor-country governments, and thus have to bear the costs of debt relief, except insofar as they might authorize the IMF to sell some of its gold or choose to shift the burden to other poor countries.

5. What about loans to purchase G-7 goods? How should they be treated in an analysis of debt relief?

The HIPC Initiative involves a 90 percent write-off of bilateral debt (Paris Club Cologne terms), and a number of countries, including the United Kingdom, have moved unilaterally to completely write off their bilateral HIPC debts. This means in a sense that the past sins of tied aid are wiped clean.

We have argued that one of debt relief's central advantages over additional new aid is the efficiency gain that comes from releasing poor countries from the kind of nonsense involved in aid contracts mandating the purchase of high-priced Western goods and services. We also support the common pool proposal (see chapter 6) to avoid unreasonable pressure on borrowers to buy from lenders at high prices. The OECD countries have pledged to end the practice of tied aid, but they have not yet applied this pledge to the two most insidious areas: technical cooperation and food aid.

6. How much good would it do the debtor countries if their debt were completely instead of partially written off? What negative effects would result in the creditor countries?

In 1999, the HIPCs paid about $8 billion in debt service on their outstanding stock of debt ($170 billion, nominal). If the debt stock were to be completely eliminated, then would the HIPCs get an immediate $8 billion-a-year windfall? We doubt it. During the past two decades (as we explain below and in table 2.1), the HIPCs have continued to receive large positive net transfers of resources—on the order of $10 billion in the second half of the 1990s—over and above their debt-service payments.

We doubt that donor governments (who would have to show in their own budgets the "cost" of the unpaid debt) and multilateral creditors (who would no longer need to make new loans to help countries pay back old loans) would refrain from cutting back, at least somewhat, on new disbursements. In fact (table 2.1) that seems to have already happened in the late 1990s, when despite higher debt relief, total transfers including debt relief not only failed to rise but actually fell. The effects on creditor countries are so tiny in financial terms that it makes no sense to quantify them. And even if the HIPCs got a full $8 billion windfall, there would be a question of equity if part of it came at the expense of other poor countries—countries that may have made better use of the resources in stimulating development and combating poverty.

7. Why is debt a worthwhile focal point when talking about development in poor countries?

Although debt relief is just another form of resource transfer to poor countries, there are (as we explain in chapter 4) good reasons to favor somewhat more debt relief over new grants or loans. Yet even complete debt relief would be only a small step toward reducing poverty and advancing development, and would be small in comparison with the potential benefits of better market access. Even with more debt relief, a seriously stepped-up rich-country effort to commit new resources is crucial.

8. Are children really dying because of the debt burden imposed on poor countries?

We think it is wrong to assert that. Why? Because the poorest, most indebted countries have generally been receiving much more aid each year than what they pay in debt service (table 2.1). In the worst cases, much of their new aid was needed to pay their debt service—but even then they ended up at least slightly ahead. There are, of course, other more fundamental reasons why children are dying, and insufficient resources is one of them.

9. Who are the central players in the debt relief debate, and who should the central players be? Who has the voice, and who should have the voice?

The big players in the debate about debt relief have been:

(1) the large donor countries—to whom much of the debt is owed, and who have the most influence in the World Bank and the IMF, the institutions that manage the HIPC program—and

(2) nongovernmental activist organizations such as Jubilee, Eurodad, and others mentioned in the text (and see the references), based mostly in those rich countries but with local affiliates in many debtor countries.

Group 1 has been a quiet but powerful player—proceeding with deeper debt relief when it became obvious that the shell game of making new grants and loans to finance debtors' debt service was undermining the logic and effectiveness of development assistance, though then only at a pace and on terms they could financially and politically "afford." Group 2 has created the persistent and healthy pressure on Group 1 needed to make the process deeper, broader, and more transparent.

10. What steps would most advance development in poor countries? Would debt relief even be one of them?
Five steps most critical to reducing poverty and advancing development in today's poor countries are:

- stable and honest government that commands the assent of the governed;

- entrepreneurship to generate good investments and jobs;

- a social contract: adequate health, education, and other social investments that provide economic and social opportunity for all;

- good access to rich-country markets; and

- an additional $50 billion a year in development assistance to build the institutions and finance the programs noted above that can help them escape poverty traps.

But these reflect the opinions of the authors; others might choose other steps.

2

The HIPC Initiative: Background and Critiques

Debt contracts are based on an expectation that debtors will repay. In the absence of such an expectation, creditors would not make loans, and all the potential benefits of intertemporal trade—of enabling savings decisions and acts of investment to be made by different persons—would be aborted. Despite this, there is a long history of debts not being serviced on the agreed terms and of debt contracts ultimately being renegotiated (box 2.1). Borrowers sometimes find themselves unable to service their debts on the contractually agreed terms or (in the case of governments) unable to do so without imposing unacceptable sacrifices on their populations. Eventually, creditors recognize this and have little recourse but to accept some losses. The HIPC Initiative, in its enhanced version, is merely the latest case in point.[1]

Sovereign lending to today's developing countries started in the 1820s, and so did the process of their defaulting on sovereign debts (Eichengreen and Lindert 1989). The consequences of defaulting were painful, but presumably paying full debt service would have been even worse. Defaulters got shut out of the international capital markets, often for extended periods. A brief summary of how default by today's developing countries fits into the long history of default on sovereign borrowing is provided in box 2.1, which ends with resolution of the 1980s Latin American debt crisis by the Brady Plan. That was directed to helping countries whose debts were primarily owed to the commercial banks. These were largely

---

1. By the time of publication, Argentina was in fact the latest case.

Box 2.1 A short history of sovereign lending and default

In 1989, then-Citicorp chairman Walter Wriston famously pronounced that "countries don't go bankrupt." This is true in the sense that there is no official international bankruptcy procedure that allows sovereign nations to free themselves from their debt obligations. Yet the implication that countries cannot default on their debts runs contrary to the historical record. Default by governments is a practice as old as the concept of credit. Throughout history, numerous countries have refused to pay their bills, unilaterally written off debts incurred by previous governments, and reduced their (internal) debt obligations by printing more money.

The first known default occurred in the fourth century BC, when 10 of 13 Greek city-states owing debts to the Delos Temple walked away from their contractual obligations. Not long after, the island of Chios, with unsustainable debts, announced that it would simply cease paying its debts until economic conditions improved. Default in ancient times often took the form of currency debasement, rather than a declaration of bankruptcy. For example, during the three Punic Wars (241-146 BC), Rome reduced the metallic content of its monetary unit from 12 ounces to half an ounce, in a series of de facto government defaults.

The practice of default continued sporadically through the Middle Ages and into modern times. Indeed, a French minister of finance contended in the 18th century that "each government should default at least once every century, in order to restore equilibrium"! During the 19th century, as the practice of lending abroad became more common, government defaults increased and most European nations partially defaulted on their debt commitments. Some defaulted multiple times; the worst culprit was Spain, with seven recorded defaults (Winkler 1933). The record in developing nations was similar: every Latin American nation without exception defaulted in the course of the 19th century.

These were not complete government bankruptcies, and they were justified by governments on a number of grounds. Some claimed unfair competitive advantage by trading partners as justification for default, others declared the debts of former governments null on taking office, and still others solicited the aid of creditors in rescheduling commitments because of economic recession.

Although the US federal government avoided outright default, many US states defaulted during this period. Many of these defaults were on Civil War debts; others were on bonds issued to failed enterprises, usually railroads or banks (Winkler 1933). Arkansas and Florida each defaulted three times during the course of the 19th century. The United States government repudiated the debts that had been incurred by Cuba while under Spanish rule at the conclusion of the Spanish-American War in 1898.

John Maynard Keynes first became famous for his opposition to the reparations obligations that were being imposed on Germany at the Versailles peace conference that followed the First World War in 1919. He argued against reparations and for the cancellation of the inter-Allied debts that had been incurred to finance the war. His objections were overruled, leading to the protracted debt difficulties that nurtured German grievances in the early 1930s. The international capital market collapsed in the wave of defaults that accompanied the Great Depression of the 1930s.

When a new international monetary order was designed at Bretton Woods in 1944, it was assumed that capital mobility had gone forever. The victors were careful to avoid the imposition of significant reparations on the vanquished at the end of the Second World War. So in the three decades following the war, sovereign defaults were rare. But the international capital market gradually revived: first in the form of foreign direct investment, then via creation of the eurodollar market; first among industrial economies, then more and more involving developing countries.

(box continues next page)

Box 2.1 *(continued)*

Defaults on bank loans became more common in the 1970s when money deposited in Western banks by members of the Organization of Petroleum Exporting Countries, as a result of successive oil shocks, prompted a surge in bank lending, especially in Latin America. US interest rate increases in the early 1980s, intended to bring inflation under control, led to a sharp increase in the cost of servicing this debt, as well as a decline in the terms of trade that eroded the ability to service debt. This prompted the Mexican moratorium of 1982, which led to the debt crisis and what is often referred to as the lost decade.

In 1989, US Treasury secretary Nicholas Brady introduced a plan to restructure the commercial bank debt owed by Latin America. Bank loans were replaced by securitized liabilities backed in effect by partial guarantes of the US government and reduced present values. The Brady Plan relieved the debt burden of countries whose indebtedness was primarily commercial. It did not cover countries whose outstanding debt was primarily to official (bilateral and multilateral) creditors, whose debts were instead handled as described in the text.

the middle-income developing countries,[2] to which the banks had been prepared to make loans during the years after the rise of the Organization of Petroleum Exporting Countries (OPEC) in the 1970s.

Most of the poorer (low-income) countries were never considered sufficiently creditworthy to be able to attract much commercial lending.[3] They were largely restricted to official finance, which came in three main forms. Two of these involved bilateral (government to government) loans: export credits, which were on more or less commercial terms; and official development assistance (ODA), which includes outright grants and loans with a grant element of at least 25 percent. The third form of official finance consists of loans from the multilateral institutions: the IMF, the World Bank, and the regional development banks, such as the African Development Bank.

Multilateral loans can in turn be divided into two types: "hard-window" loans, where borrowers' interest cost is related to the institution's own cost of borrowing, and "soft-window" or "concessional" loans. The latter are much more highly subsidized and are therefore directly funded by contributions that donor governments make to the banks' soft windows—

---

2. We use the World Bank's classification to distinguish between low-income and middle-income developing countries. Low-income countries had per capita GNP at or below $755 in 2000 (measured at market exchange rates); middle-income ones had per capita GNP between $755 and $9,266. Middle-income countries are split into lower-middle-income ones, with per capita GNP below $2,955, and upper-middle-income ones with a higher per capita GNP. Appendix B lists all the countries with a population of more than 1.5 million in each category.

3. Except for a few countries like Côte d'Ivoire, and for "enclave" extractive sectors, like minerals, oil, and plantation agriculture in a wider range of countries.

Figure 2.1   ODA loans to sub-Saharan Africa, 1970-99

millions of 1995
constant dollars

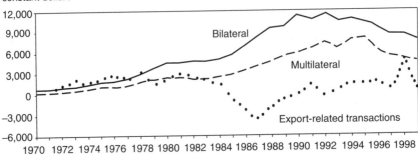

Note: Export-related transactions include official export credits, loans to national private exporters (i.e., official loans to private export credit agencies to partially finance export credits extended by them to developing countries), and interest subsidies to national private exporters of DAC countries (subsidies to reduce the interest rate charged on private export credits).

Source: Organization for Economic Cooperation and Development, Development Assistance Committee (DAC) reporting system.

such as the International Development Association (IDA) in the case of the World Bank.

As is shown in figure 2.1, official loans to sub-Saharan Africa—which mostly consists of low-income countries, although there are also of course low-income countries elsewhere—increased rather gradually in both nominal and real terms until the early 1980s. At that time, many of these countries began to experience debt-servicing problems akin to those being confronted by their middle-income peers. Because their creditors were largely official institutions rather than private commercial banks, these problems were handled differently than those of the middle-income countries. The Paris Club was the main instrument used, initially simply to reschedule official debt.[4] But donors (especially the Europeans) more and more began to appreciate that low-income countries were likely to have difficulty servicing loans on the near-commercial terms characteristic of export credits, and so in the mid-1980s they phased out such lending and replaced it with higher levels of lower-interest ODA loans.

Multilateral lending also expanded vigorously during the 1980s. From the IMF and World Bank alone (not including the regional development banks), lending increased from less than $1 billion to about $6 billion

---

4. The Paris Club is an ad hoc group of official creditors that seeks to coordinate the restructuring of official bilateral debt when sovereign debtors encounter debt-servicing problems. The club has 19 permanent members, and other creditors are invited to participate on a case-by-case basis. Since its first meeting in 1956, the club has negotiated 336 agreements encompassing 76 debtor countries.

Figure 2.2 World Bank and IMF loan disbursements to low-income countries, 1970-99

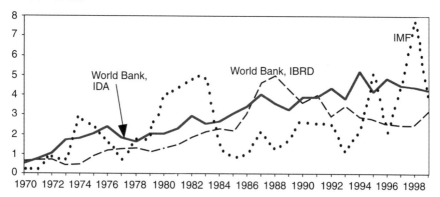

billions of 1995
constant dollars

IBRD = International Bank for Reconstruction and Development
IDA = International Development Association

Source: World Bank, *Global Development Finance* CD-ROM, 2001.

annually (in constant 1995 dollars), as is shown in figure 2.2. Lending by IDA tended to increase relative to that by the International Bank for Reconstruction and Development (IBRD, the hard window of the World Bank) after 1986, again reflecting an attempt to ease the terms confronting low-income countries. IMF lending more and more took the form of concessional lending from what was first called the Trust Fund, then the Structural Adjustment Facility, and then the Enhanced Structural Adjustment Facility; in the era of the enhanced HIPC Initiative, it was renamed yet again as the Poverty Reduction and Growth Facility.

In consequence, although low-income countries outside Asia grew much less in the 1980s than they had in the 1970s, they did not suffer the same precipitous decline in access to external credits as did the middle-income countries of Latin America. Although the countries subsequently labeled HIPCs did suffer a decline in "net transfers on debt" (which is loan disbursements minus debt service payments), total resource transfers remained positive for the group as a whole. Indeed, that was true for each individual HIPC except Côte d'Ivoire, which had borrowed more in the more costly commercial market. That is, the decline in debt transfers was fully compensated for by an increase in grants in the 1980s, and more than fully in the early (though not in the late) 1990s (see table 2.1). Most of these countries did not participate in the negotiations over commercial bank debt restructuring in the middle to late 1980s. In short, for the poorer countries there was no visible 1980s "debt crisis."

Table 2.1 Resource flows to HIPCs and all developing countries, 1980-99 (billions of constant 1995 dollars)

	HIPCs					All developing countries			
Flow	1980-84	1985-89	1990-94	1995-99	Flow	1980-84	1985-89	1990-94	1995-99
PPG disbursements	14.4	12.7	9.7	9.2	PPG disbursements	148.6	138.0	169.9	285.3
PPG debt service	6.8	8.4	7.0	8.8	PPG debt service	118.4	165.6	168.5	282.6
PNG disbursements	0.8	0.6	0.4	0.5	PNG disbursements	23.8	10.9	38.9	103.0
PNG debt service	1.1	1.1	0.7	0.7	PNG debt service	27.0	21.5	26.0	84.4
Net transfers on debt	7.3	3.9	2.4	0.1	Net transfers on debt	26.9	-38.2	14.2	21.3
Grants	6.7	10.1	14.5	11.6	Grants	23.7	32.2	50.3	45.6
Total net transfers	14.0	14.0	16.9	11.7	Total net transfers	50.6	-6.0	64.5	66.9

PPG = public or publicly guaranteed
PNG = private nonguaranteed

Note: Total net transfers are the sum of disbursements and grants less debt service. Net transfers on debt are loan disbursements less debt service.

Source: World Bank, *Global Development Finance* CD-ROM, 2001.

Table 2.2 Growth in HIPCs and other developing countries, 1980-99 (percent per year)

	HIPCs				Low-income countries				Middle-income countries			
Measure of growth	1980-84	1985-89	1990-94	1995-99	1980-84	1985-89	1990-94	1995-99	1980-84	1985-89	1990-94	1995-99
GDP growth	1.1	2.7	0.9	4.8	4.6	5.1	2.0	3.9	2.9	3.6	2.7	3.6
Population growth	2.7	2.7	2.6	2.5	2.3	2.3	2.1	2.0	1.6	1.7	1.4	1.2
Per capita GDP growth	-1.6	0.0	-1.7	2.3	2.3	2.8	-0.1	1.9	1.3	1.9	1.3	2.4

Sources: World Bank, *Global Development Finance* CD-ROM, 2001; HIPC Debt Sustainability Analyses.

The Heavily Indebted Poor Countries

However, the group of countries that eventually became the HIPCs already exhibited symptoms of increasing and potentially unmanageable debt in the 1980s. Debt-export and debt-GNP ratios were already higher in the HIPCs in the 1980s than in other developing countries[5] (figure 2.3). The comparison is less striking in terms of debt service because of the high proportion of concessional loans with relatively long grace periods before debt-service payments kick in, but the debt-service ratio was still high.[6] So the first common characteristic of the HIPCs is that they were already heavily indebted more than a decade ago.

The second common characteristic of the countries included in the HIPC Initiative is of course that they are poor; because their economies have not grown much, their peoples are generally as poor today as they were two decades ago. Of the total current population of HIPCs of 615 million, almost half live on less than $1 a day (World Bank 2000b, 9). With slow growth (see table 2.2), the number and even the proportion of poor people have increased in the past two decades. Real GDP per capita was lower in 1999 in 10 of the 21 HIPCs for which there are data than it was in 1960. It is because of their poverty—and the fact that poverty was getting worse rather than better, at least until the late 1990s—that the world feels a special concern for these countries.[7]

A third common characteristic of the HIPCs has been their high receipts of ODA. Gross transfers in the form of grants and loans from bilateral and multilateral donors and creditors in the past two decades amounted to about $445 billion in constant 1995 dollars. On average, net transfers (gross transfers minus debt service paid by them) to the HIPCs were about 10 percent of their GDP in the 1990s, representing as much as 60 percent of government revenue[8] and financing most public investment. This compares to an average for all other developing countries in the past

---

5. All figures, unless otherwise noted, are derived from the World Bank's *Global Development Finance* and *World Development Indicators* 2001 CD-ROMs, and are in constant 1995 US dollars (deflating by the US wholesale price index). When referring to HIPCs, we generally mean the 38 of the 41 countries deemed eligible for the HIPC Initiative as of December 2000 for which there are data (data are consistently unavailable for Liberia, Myanmar, and Somalia). Comoros was added to the list of eligible countries in 2001.

6. E.g., the concessional loans from the World Bank's IDA window have a 10-year grace period. This increased the debt-service ratio in the late 1990s as grace periods from the high level of lending in the 1980s ended.

7. The great majority of the world's poor live outside the HIPCs, in China (350 million), India (525 million), the Latin American countries (60 million), and elsewhere. Some of those countries are more able to raise and allocate resources internally to attack the poverty of their people.

8. Government revenue data are limited, and available for only 19 HIPCs in the 1990s.

Figure 2.3 Debt ratios of HIPCs and other developing countries
(percent)

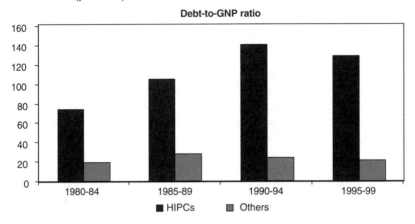

Debt-to-GNP ratio

■ HIPCs   ■ Others

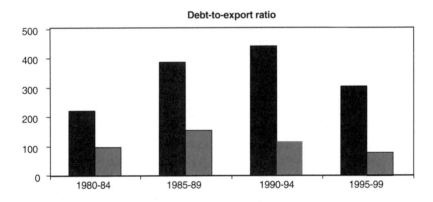

Debt-to-export ratio

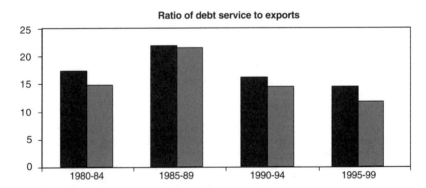

Ratio of debt service to exports

Source: World Bank, *Global Development Finance* CD-ROM, 2001.

two decades of about 2 percent of GDP. Transfers often exceeded the government's own revenue collection. In some extreme cases, gross transfers were more than 60 percent of GDP (though only in tiny São Tomé and Principe have they exceeded the proportion in eastern Germany after reunification).[9]

The high levels of development assistance and the stagnation in exports and government revenue (which resulted from the low growth) combined to produce a more and more unmanageable stock of debt. The debt of the HIPC Initiative-eligible countries grew from about $59 billion in 1980 to $170 billion in 1999, which increased the average debt-to-export ratio from 199 to 414 percent and the average debt-to-GNP ratio from 31 percent in 1981 to 103 percent in 1999. The increase in annual debt-service obligations was far more muted, owing to the increasing levels of concessionality and the accumulation of annual arrears, from $7 billion in 1980 to about $9 billion in 1999. The debt-service ratio actually declined in the 1990s but was still a high 18 percent of exports in 1999.

This outcome was vastly different from that anticipated in the early days of foreign aid. For example, the Pearson Commission, which issued its report in 1969 and first formalized an aid target, suggested that industrial countries should commit themselves to a target of giving 0.7 percent of their GNP as foreign aid. The commission assumed that this would be a temporary effort and that the need for aid would be winding down by the turn of the century.[10] It was taken for granted that countries receiving aid would make sufficiently good investments to enable them to service low-interest loans without difficulty. But things did not follow that path in the countries that are now HIPCs, including in most of sub-Saharan Africa (Lancaster 1999).

Recent Debt Relief Initiatives

By the end of the 1980s, the accumulation of official public debt on the part of many low-income countries was more and more troubling donors. Given the continuing needs of recipient countries, including for help in strengthening health and education systems and other programs of human development, donors sought ways to sustain high positive net transfers, despite the growing volume of debt service to donors and to multilaterals now being paid by borrowing countries.

---

9. Transfers from west to east averaged $100 billion for the first half of the 1990s, representing approximately 100 percent of eastern Germany's GDP and 7 percent of western Germany's (Wurzel 2001).

10. The Commission on International Development was headed by former Canadian prime minister Lester Pearson (Pearson 1969). One of the authors of this study served as a research assistant on the staff of this commission.

Figure 2.4 Evolution of ODA disbursements from EU countries, 1980-99

millions of 1995
constant dollars

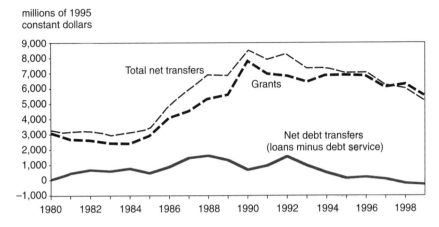

Source: Organization for Economic Cooperation and Development, Development Assistance Committee reporting system.

One step was a foretaste of the current proposal that IDA switch some of its lending to grants: The European governments switched away from already highly concessional loans to straight grants, beginning in the mid-1980s and continuing into the 1990s. Figure 2.4 displays disbursements of grants and net loans from EU countries. It shows that in the middle of the 1990s the net debt transfer turned negative. However, this was for a long time offset by the increasing level of grants, so that the net transfer remained as large as before. Only in the mid-1990s did net transfers start to decline, although even then they remained positive.

In addition, bilateral donors began negotiating formal programs of official debt relief. These began in earnest in 1989 and intensified in the 1990s (box 2.2). Initial rounds were confined to a reduction in debt service, with donors reluctant to forgive debt stock—perhaps in an effort to preserve the principle of the sanctity of debt contracts, or perhaps because of accounting conventions. Whatever the reason, the consequence was a ballooning in the value of what had often started as nonconcessional export credits. By the mid-1990s, however, official donors were providing some countries the option of debt stock cancellation. The debt relief possibilities were directly linked to IMF programs and were deliberately ad hoc and case by case. These first rounds of official debt relief attracted relatively little public interest or attention.

The switch of bilateral donors from loans to grants, combined with the low level of private lending to most low-income countries, meant that by the mid-1990s an increasing proportion of the debt of the poorest countries

Box 2.2 Debt initiatives

- *Special Program of Assistance for Africa, 1987:* Informal donor association managed by the World Bank to provide bilateral debt relief, IDA credits for IBRD debt service relief, and funding for commercial debt buybacks. Available to African IDA-only borrowers with ratios of debt service to exports above 30 percent (initially 21 countries).
- *Paris Club: Toronto terms, 1988:* First agreement by Paris Club creditors to implement new treatment on the debt of low-income countries. The level of reduction was a uniform 33.33 percent.[1]
- *Brady Plan, 1989:* The World Bank and IMF facilitated debt and debt service reductions by commercial bank creditors. Most Brady deals went to middle-income countries.
- *IDA Debt Reduction Facility, 1989:* Established to restructure and buy back commercial debt with IDA credits (average 88 percent discount). Available to low-income countries (heavily indebted IDA-only borrowers). Funded from IBRD net income transfer.
- *Paris Club: Houston terms, 1990:* Agreement to implement a new treatment of the debt of the *lower-middle-income* countries. Houston terms had three components: repayment periods lengthened to or beyond 15 years and ODA repayment periods lengthened up to 20 years with a maximum 10-year grace period; ODA rescheduled at a concessional rate; and the introduction of bilateral debt swaps.
- *Paris Club: London ("enhanced Toronto") terms, 1991:* Debt service reduced 50 percent on nonconcessional bilateral debt (12-year grace period, 30-year maturity).
- *Paris Club: Naples terms, 1995:* Debt service reduced 67 percent on nonconcessional bilateral debt (16-year grace period, 40-year maturity). Option of debt stock cancellation (5 stock deals processed).[2]
- *HIPC Initiative (HIPC I), 1996:* Debt stock reduction to bring debt-export ratio under 200 percent for 41 heavily indebted poor countries. Participation of multilateral creditors.
- *Paris Club: Lyon terms, 1996:* Agreement within HIPC framework for 80 percent relief on nonconcessional bilateral debt for HIPC Initiative-eligible countries.
- *Enhanced HIPC Initiative (HIPC II), 1999:* Increased stock reductions to bring debt of HIPCs to under 150 percent debt-export ratio. Interim debt-service reduction between decision and completion points. Relief conditioned on the completion of comprehensive Poverty Reduction Strategy Papers.
- *Paris Club: Cologne terms, 1999:* Agreement within HIPC framework, non-ODA credits canceled up to 90 percent or more if necessary in the context of the HIPC Initiative (including topping up). ODA credits rescheduled at an interest rate at least as favorable as the original concessional interest rate applying to these loans (40-year terms, with 16-year grace period and progressive repayment).

---

1. Paris Club debt reduction decisions are made according to five principles: case-by-case decision making, consensus, conditionality (the existence and continuation of an IMF program), solidarity, and comparability of treatment.

2. The option of stock treatments was and is implemented "on a case-by-case basis, for countries having established a satisfactory track record with both the Paris Club and IMF and for which there is sufficient confidence in their ability to respect the debt agreement" (Paris Club Web site, http://www.clubdeparis.org).

Figure 2.5 Breakdown of debt by creditor, nominal debt stock, 1999

Heavily indebted poor countries ($170 billion)

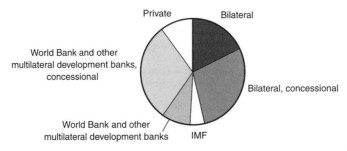

Other low-income countries ($270 billion)

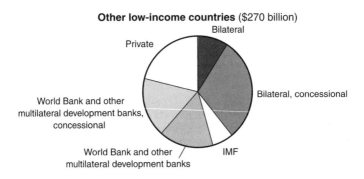

All developing countries ($1,620 billion)

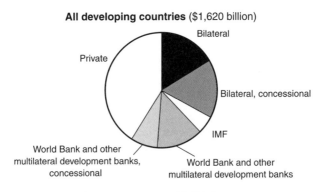

Source: World Bank, *Global Development Finance* CD-ROM, 2001.

was owed to official multilateral creditors, notably the IMF and World Bank. This was especially true of the HIPCs. Figure 2.5 shows the debt of the HIPCs, other low-income countries, and all developing countries broken down by creditor. It shows that debt owed to multilateral institutions represented 44 percent of the HIPCs' total debt and 25 percent of the debt of all developing countries, whereas publicly guaranteed commercial debt made up only 10 percent of HIPC debt but 42 percent of developing-country debt. It became evident that the overall debt burden of the poorest countries, especially the HIPCs, could not easily be handled while continuing to treat the multilaterals as preferred creditors (Martin 1997).

The multilaterals have always been treated as "preferred creditors" in the sense that their credit was recognized, by debtors and all other creditors, as senior to all other debt—first in line for repayment, and payable in full even if other debt cannot be serviced. Because the multilaterals are preferred creditors, failing to repay them means a debtor will be liable to be cut off from all other debt financing, including for short-term trade credits. In the official donor community, defaulting to the multilaterals is seen as virtually tantamount to withdrawal from the international community of nations. So for both financial and political reasons, the official donors went to great lengths to help ensure that a poor debtor country (other than a rogue state) did not fall into arrears to the preferred multilateral creditors.

The first HIPC program was negotiated in 1996 and was notable for two reasons. First, it not only explicitly emphasized debt-stock reduction, but it keyed the extent of debt-stock reduction to what would be needed in a particular country to achieve "debt sustainability." This was in contrast to previous relief under the Paris Club, where (for example) the Naples terms provided a uniform 67 percent reduction for all countries that qualified. Instead, an attempt was made to calculate what would be needed to enable each country to exit the process of constant rescheduling and resume normal relations with its creditors, where it serviced all its remaining debt, that is, where it achieved debt sustainability. The benchmark was set at 200 percent debt-export ratio; countries above that level could become eligible.

Second, for the first time debt relief included reduction of debt owed to the multilateral institutions—the IMF, the World Bank, and the regional and subregional development banks.[11] This was judged necessary because the switch from loans to grants by the bilaterals meant that a large and growing share of debt service was being paid to the multilaterals. However, partly to maintain this formal status as preferred creditors, the institutions were not to write off the debt owed to them on their own books. Instead, the debt service owed to them was to be paid to them through special trust funds created for that purpose. The trust funds are financed by direct contributions from governments and, in the case of the World Bank, by transfer of some of its net income from its ordinary (non-IDA) lending.

---

11. See appendix A for a complete list of multilateral institutions participating in the HIPC Initiative.

The technical design of the original HIPC program was conceived by IMF and World Bank staff (and approved by the shareholders through the boards of the two institutions) along traditional lines of conditionality. Debtor countries would become eligible for the HIPC program (reach the "decision point") only when they had maintained stable macroeconomic conditions under approved IMF programs for at least 6 years; and would receive a permanent reduction in their official debt stock (reach the "completion point") only after another 3 years of satisfactory policy.

The World Bank and IMF predicted in 1996 that 20 of the 40 countries then eligible would eventually reach the completion point, and that the HIPC Initiative would provide a total debt-stock reduction of $8.2 billion (about 20 percent of their outstanding debt) in terms of net present value (NPV).[12] After nearly 3 years in the process, however, only 6 countries— Bolivia, Burkina Faso, Côte d'Ivoire, Guyana, Mozambique, and Uganda—had reached the decision point, and only Uganda had reached the completion point. The official creditors—under strong pressure from the Jubilee movement, and frustrated with the stringent eligibility requirements and slowness of the process—came back together in 1999 and agreed to an "enhanced" HIPC framework to provide more and faster debt relief for more countries, mainly in Africa.

The Enhanced HIPC Framework

The enhanced HIPC framework was agreed to by the G-7 at their July 1999 summit at Cologne in Germany and endorsed at the annual meetings of the IMF and World Bank that September. The terms of the enhanced framework reduce the time period before the decision point to less than 3 years, reduce eligibility standards to allow more relief to more countries, and alter the delivery structure to provide for greater debt-service relief between decision and completion points. Under the enhanced initiative, a country is eligible if:

■ its per capita income is low: access is limited to countries entitled to borrow on IDA-only terms from the World Bank and from the IMF's Poverty Reduction and Growth Facility;[13]

---

12. All NPV calculations are from the World Bank and are made using a conventional 7 percent discount rate. Projections of the total relief provided by the HIPC Initiative continued to change, as countries' individual timelines and eligibility requirements were analyzed. By 1999, before the enhanced HIPC Initiative, the projection for relief under HIPC I had increased to $12.5 billion for 29 countries.

13. As we discuss in chapter 5, some low-income countries, including Indonesia, Nigeria, and Pakistan, are not IDA only because they have (or has) some access to private capital markets, and thus are not eligible for the HIPC Initiative.

- it can demonstrate a good track record of reform (in principle over 3 years) at the time when the program is approved (the decision point);

- either the ratio of its net present value of debt to exports exceeds 150 percent; or

- for countries with open economies (a minimum 30 percent export-GNP ratio) and substantial tax revenue (a minimum of 15 percent of GNP), the ratio of the NPV of debt to tax revenue exceeds 250 percent.[14]

Countries begin receiving debt-service relief from multilateral creditors as soon as they reach the decision point; that is, the annual flows of debt service due are immediately reduced. The actual debt-stock reductions are delayed until the completion point.

In contrast to the original program, conditioned primarily on macroeconomic stability, the enhanced HIPC program also puts new emphasis on countries' demonstrating a firm commitment to reducing poverty by using resources that would otherwise have been used for debt service. In an effort to make sure that the released resources are in fact used for that purpose, eligibility under the enhanced framework is directly linked to agreement on a new Poverty Reduction Strategy Paper. Reflecting the donors' current enthusiasm for participation, this is to be drawn up through a process of dialogue primarily with civil society groups and other domestic stakeholders, with the aim of ensuring local ownership of a development program strongly focused on poverty reduction.

Under public pressure generated by the Jubilee movement, the IMF and World Bank pressed hard to get a lot of countries to their decision points by the end of 2000.[15] As a result, 12 additional countries were approved for decision points in the final two months of 2000, for a total of 22 countries. Chad reached its decision point in early 2001. The first 23 HIPCs will be entitled to nominal debt relief of $33.9 billion ($20.5 in NPV terms) when they reach their completion points. Annual debt-service savings during 2001-03 for those countries are estimated at $1.1 billion, in comparison with debt service paid in 1998-99 of $9.4 billion (World Bank 2001a, table 2).[16] The reduction in debt service as compared to debt service *actually owed* is substantially larger, at $2.4 billion (with the

---

14. This option was included to avoid the possibility that some countries with high ratios of exports to GDP would fail to qualify despite having a debt that was very burdensome to service. The option had in fact been developed and applied (to Côte d'Ivoire) before 1999.

15. Not all the nongovernmental organizations (NGOs) in the Jubilee movement supported the rush to maximize the number of countries getting to the decision point by the end of 2000. At least one NGO reports that in one or two countries their local counterparts feared that the benefits would go only to corrupt governments and insider cliques.

16. Drop the Debt (2001, 9) quantifies the savings as only $0.7 billion, on the basis of a comparison with 2001-05 instead of 2001-03.

difference being the extent to which HIPCs were failing to pay debt service and thus building up arrears). A further 2 countries, Ethiopia and Ghana, reached decision points by February 2002, for a total of 25. Of these, 4 countries have by now reached completion points under the enhanced framework and have actually had their debt stock reduced.

Forty-two countries have now been identified as eligible for the HIPC Initiative. These are shown in table 2.3, divided into five groups. The first consists of the 4 countries that have already reached completion point: Bolivia, Mozambique, Tanzania, and Uganda. The second consists of the 21 other countries that have already reached decision point; all except 3 (Guyana, Honduras, and Nicaragua) are African countries. Third are 12 countries, all in Africa except Myanmar, that are expected to reach decision point in the future; 9 of these are suffering internal conflicts, which is likely to preclude their rapid establishment of the good track record of economic management needed to qualify them for decision point.

The fourth category consists of 4 countries that now satisfy the conditions for the HIPC status but are unlikely to need HIPC relief because "traditional mechanisms" of debt relief, meaning the terms now on offer from the Paris Club, are expected to reduce their debt ratios below the critical level (90 percent of both Angola's and Vietnam's large debt burden is owed to bilateral creditors). In the last category is just Lao PDR, which has been tempted by Japanese offers of new aid not to seek HIPC relief. Japan is the one donor country that is reluctant to commit to the HIPC Initiative; instead, it would prefer countries to preserve the appearance of the sanctity of debt contracts by continuing to take on ever more unserviceable debt to maintain the fiction of servicing their existing debt.

Table 2.4 presents debt data for the 42 HIPCs. The top part of the table presents data for the 24 countries that had reached decision point by January 2002 (the first two categories identified above, with the exception of Ghana); the bottom part deals with the remaining 18 countries. The first column shows the nominal value of publicly guaranteed debt outstanding in 1999 before the enhanced HIPC Initiative started. This varied from a mere $294 million for tiny São Tomé and Principe (population 140,000) to $20.8 billion for Vietnam with its 80 million people (for a total of $170 billion). Because most of this debt is highly concessional, however, the NPV of the debt, shown in the second column, is in most cases substantially less than its nominal value, totaling about $130 billion for the 42 HIPCs.

The third column of table 2.4 shows the first of the traditional measures of how burdensome the debt is: the ratio of debt (specifically, of the NPV of debt) to exports. HIPC I aimed to reduce this ratio to no more than 200 percent, on the argument that history showed that larger values than that usually proved to be unsustainable; HIPC II reduced the target to 150 percent, to allow some leeway for debt burdens to increase in the

Table 2.3 Heavily indebted poor countries

Completion point (4)	Decision point (21)		Future decision points (12)	(Potentially) sustainable cases (4)	Not seeking relief (1)
Bolivia	Benin	Madagascar	Burundi[a]	Angola[a]	Lao PDR
Mozambique	Burkina Faso	Malawi	Central African Republic[a]	Kenya	
Tanzania	Cameroon	Mali	Comoros	Vietnam	
Uganda	Chad	Mauritania	Congo, Democratic Republic of[a]	Yemen	
	Ethiopia	Nicaragua	Congo, Republic of[a]		
	Gambia	Niger	Côte d'Ivoire		
	Ghana	Rwanda[a]	Liberia[a]		
	Guinea	São Tomé and Principe	Myanmar[a]		
	Guinea-Bissau[a]	Senegal	Sierra Leone[a]		
	Guyana	Zambia	Somalia[a]		
	Honduras		Sudan[a]		
			Togo		

a. Affected by conflict.

Source: World Bank HIPC Web site, http://www.worldbank.org/hipc.

Table 2.4 Debt statistics for HIPCs

Countries that have reached decision point

Country	Debt out-standing (nominal)	Debt out-standing (NPV)	NPV of debt-to-exports	NPV of debt-to-GNP	Ratio of debt service to exports	Ratio of debt service to GNP	Estimated total relief (nominal)[a]	Estimated total relief (NPV)[a]	Ratio of NPV relief-debt (percent)	Estimated ratio of debt service to exports	Estimated ratio of debt service to GDP
Benin	1,419	950	148	40	11	3	460	265	28	9.4	1.4
Bolivia[b]	4,606	2,974	193	37	32	6	2,060	1,302	44	12.1	3.0
Burkina Faso	1,499	631	158	25	16	3	700	398	63	9.2	1.1
Cameroon	7,802	6,601	292	76	24	6	2,000	1,260	19	8.2	2.5
Chad	1,142	656	208	43	10	2	260	157	24	8.9	1.3
Ethiopia	5,551	3,529	374	55	17	3	n.a.	n.a.	n.a.	n.a.	n.a.
Gambia	453	258	103	67	9	6	90	67	26	8.5	3.1
Guinea	3,375	2,415	294	71	16	4	800	545	23	8.7	3.5
Guinea-Bissau	944	709	1,222	348	16	5	790	416	59	5.4	1.7
Guyana	1,214	867	n.a.	140	n.a.	17	1,030	585	67	5.2	7.1
Honduras	4,288	3,296	122	63	14	7	900	556	17	5.8	3.1
Madagascar	4,358	2,943	304	80	17	5	1,500	814	28	5.5	1.3
Malawi	2,608	1,482	246	84	11	4	1,000	643	43	10.5	2.9
Mali	3,038	1,429	193	57	14	4	870	523	37	8.1	2.3
Mauritania	2,072	1,567	422	170	28	11	1,100	622	40	13.4	4.5
Mozambique[b]	5,019	2,731	167	28	20	3	4,300	1,970	72	4.8	1
Nicaragua	6,413	5,541	475	271	16	9	4,500	3,267	59	13.4	5.2
Niger	1,604	1,089	362	55	17	3	900	521	48	14.1	1.9
Rwanda	1,261	696	655	36	30	2	810	452	65	7.7	0.6
São Tomé and Príncipe	294	190	1,285	450	29	10	200	97	51	7.4	4.6
Senegal	3,618	2,495	169	53	16	5	850	488	20	7.4	3.1
Tanzania[b]	6,385	4,613	370	53	16	2	3,000	2,026	44	8.6	1.4
Uganda[b]	3,217	1,748	225	27	24	3	1,950	1,003	57	4.7	0.7
Zambia	4,566	4,074	548	172	47	15	3,820	2,499	61	11.4	3.7

Countries still to be considered

Country	PPG debt outstanding (nominal)	PPG debt outstanding (NPV)	NPV of debt-to-exports	NPV of debt-to-GNP	Ratio of debt service to exports	Ratio of debt service to GNP
Angola	9,248	7,226	133	244	20	37
Burundi	1,062	636	1,009	90	43	4
Central African Republic	854	528	343	51	11	2
Comoros	182	120	251	62	15	4
Congo, Democratic Republic of	8,600	8,060	n.a.	n.a.	n.a.	n.a.
Congo, Republic of	3,961	3,751	209	226	0	0
Côte d'Ivoire	10,319	9,509	172	91	18	10
Ghana	5,957	4,302	164	56	18	6
Kenya	5,517	4,358	163	42	22	6
Lao PDR	2,524	1,385	289	99	8	3
Liberia	1,371	1,318	n.a.	n.a.	n.a.	n.a.
Myanmar	5,333	3,992	n.a.	n.a.	n.a.	n.a.
Sierra Leone	1,133	806	1,119	124	29	3
Somalia	2,013	1,792	n.a.	n.a.	n.a.	n.a.
Sudan	9,567	8,970	1,018	102	6	1
Togo	1,345	1,010	194	73	7	3
Vietnam	20,884	19,458	136	68	10	5
Yemen	4,138	3,188	81	52	4	2

n.a. = not available

NPV = net present value

PPG = public or publicly guaranteed

a. Estimated relief includes enhanced HIPC and all traditional debt reduction mechanisms (Paris Club, etc.).

b. Reached completion point.

Source: World Bank, *Global Development Finance* CD-ROM, 2001 (GDF). The 2nd through 7th columns are for 1999. The NPV of publicly guaranteed debt for non-decision-point countries is calculated by discounting the nominal PPG figures by the ratio of nominal to net present value of total outstanding debt, table A1.4. The 8th and 9th columns are from World Bank, "HIPC Initiative: Status of Country Cases Considered under the Initiative," October 2001. The 11th and 12th columns are from World Bank, "Financial Impact of the HIPC Initiative," October 2001.

future without pushing countries straight back into unsustainability. It can be seen that almost all the countries were at more than 150 percent and most were at more than 200 percent, with São Tomé and Principe the highest at a staggering 1,285 percent. The fourth column shows the ratio of the NPV of debt to GNP, the other traditional measure of the burden of a debt stock, where 40 percent is a traditional rule of thumb for the maximum comfortable level and 60 percent for severe indebtedness. The majority of the countries were way over even the higher level, with São Tomé and Principe again the highest at 450 percent.

The next two columns of table 2.4 look at the burden of debt service, first in terms of the debt-service ratio (the percentage of export revenue that is needed to service the debt) and then in terms of the percentage of GNP used in servicing the foreign debt. One thinks of 15 percent as a normal figure for the debt-service ratio and 25 percent as a high figure. Despite the concessional nature of most debt, 24 of the 39 countries for which data are available had debt-service ratios exceeding 15 percent, and 5 of these had ratios of more than 25 percent. If a normal level of foreign debt is 40 percent of GNP and servicing concessional debt costs about 5 percent of the debt stock each year, then a norm for the ratio of debt service to GNP would be 2 percent,[17] a level exceeded by no fewer than 36 of the 39 HIPCs for which data are available.

These data leave little reason to doubt that all the HIPCs, except Yemen and perhaps Benin, were overindebted by at least one measure, often severely so. How much does enhanced HIPC promise to remedy that? This question can only be answered for the countries that have already reached the decision point and therefore have received a quantitative promise of debt relief.

The last five columns in the upper panel of table 2.4 therefore show statistics about the relief that countries have been promised under the HIPC Initiative. First is the figure for the nominal value of debt relief (including that provided through traditional mechanisms like the Paris Club as well as the initiative itself), and then its net present value. The next column divides the NPV of debt relief by the NPV of debt to calculate the percentage of the debt burden that is being relieved, which varies from 17 percent in Honduras to 72 percent in Mozambique. The penultimate column shows the estimated post-HIPC Initiative debt service ratio, which is everywhere brought down to less than 15 percent and is often substantially less.[18] The final column shows the estimated post-HIPC Initiative percentage of GNP that will be spent on servicing foreign debt, which varies rather substantially from a low of 0.6 percent in Rwanda to a high of 5.3 percent in Guyana.

---

17. A level that we subsequently argue would be reasonable as well.

18. The estimates come from World Bank and IMF (2001a).

Critiques of the Enhanced HIPC Initiative

If the IMF and World Bank hoped that the enhanced HIPC Initiative would evoke a chorus of praise from Jubilee for their response to its calls for debt relief, they must have been sadly disappointed. Within months of announcing to the world that they had slightly overachieved their target of having half the HIPCs reach decision points by the end of 2000, a flood of papers with titles like *Rethinking HIPC Debt Sustainability* (Eurodad 2001), *Still Waiting for the Jubilee* (Roodman 2001), *Debt Relief: Still Failing the Poor* (Oxfam 2001), *Reality Check: The Need for Deeper Debt Cancellation and the Fight Against HIV/AIDS* (Drop the Debt 2001) and *HIPC—Flogging a Dead Process* (Pettifor, Thomas, and Telatin 2001) were rolling off the press.

The many critiques of the current debt relief initiative can be put into two broad categories. These represent two different perspectives on the underlying causes of the failure of development assistance programs in the poorest countries. The first is perhaps more prevalent among Group A and the second among Group B, but it is possible to see some validity in both (as we do).

The "foreign aid down the rathole" argument goes as follows.[19] Debt relief and other forms of aid have been too great and too easy to get. Recipient governments are often wasteful and corrupt. Even in the best cases of reasonably adequate governance, aid and debt relief simply relieve countries' immediate budget constraint, allowing them to persist with bad economic policies. The solution is tough conditionality on good macroeconomic policy and on good governance, and if conditionality does not work, a high level of *selectivity*, rewarding countries with debt relief and new aid only when they have demonstrated adequate performance in economic management and governance.

The official donors and creditors share some blame for providing too many loans (and grants), driven by a combination of political and commercial motives (bilateral donors) and bureaucratic incentives combined with overeager professionalism and lack of accountability (IMF and World Bank staffs). They need to become more disciplined and selective in providing debt relief and in making loans and grants.

The second is the "poverty trap" argument.[20] Under this argument, debt reduction is too small and tied to conditionality that is onerous and misguided. Given poor countries' often troubled colonial and postcolonial histories, ethnic fragmentation, high burdens of tropical disease, depen-

---

19. This argument is represented by Easterly (1999), by Thomas (2001), and in some measure by Burnside and Dollar (2000).

20. This argument is represented by Sachs et al. (1999), Pettifor, Thomas, and Telatin (2001), and Oxfam (2001).

dence on primary commodities with declining and unstable prices, and often small size, debt relief and other forms of aid have been far from adequate to allow them to escape poverty and put them onto a growth path.[21] The problem is not too much but too little aid, and way too much existing debt. Of course there has been some waste, but incompetent and corrupt government is an outcome as much as a cause of poverty and underdevelopment. Moreover, the structural adjustment and other economic policies pushed by official creditors have been inappropriate for such countries, making matters worse rather than better, and rewarding the elites while burdening the poor.

From this perspective, much more of the blame goes to creditors and donors. Too much of the lending was wasteful and *inefficient*, sustaining donors' own bureaucracies and financing purchases of their goods and the use of their high-cost consultants. Worst of all, much was politically motivated, incurred in dubious situations that call its legitimacy into question. Loans were made to rulers more concerned to increase their personal or family wealth than to promote any concept of the social good. Loans were made to purchase armaments for which there was no pressing national need; indeed, these arms were sometimes used to suppress the population. Lending financed theft and capital flight by the elite and the corruption associated with building white elephants rather than capital assets that were of value to the population of the borrowing countries. Should countries be expected to service such debt? Does elementary justice not demand that it be canceled?

Some who focus on this perspective go on to argue that well-financed international creditors such as the IMF and World Bank should take their losses and write off the bad loans.[22] To impose more future accountability on official creditors, there should be an independent bankruptcy procedure—where the creditors are not the arbiters of losses for which they are partly responsible, as is now the case.[23] The government donors, especially the stingier United States, should be much more generous, with *additional* contributions to finance the debt write-off as well as new aid. Debt relief and new aid should be linked to programs that ensure that the poor have voice and power in the way government allocates new resources, and indeed all its resources. The solutions, in other words, are

---

21. Birdsall and Hamoudi (2002) identify a group of 34 "most commodity dependent" countries (out of a set of 137 countries, using data from Statistics Canada's World Trade Analyzer). Of these, 21 are HIPCs. Further, of the current HIPCs, those less dependent on commodities have performed better and reached the decision point faster (10 of the 12 HIPCs yet to reach the decision point are in Birdsall and Hamoudi's "most commodity dependent" category).

22. This is a central argument of Roodman (2001).

23. This is the position taken by Pettifor, Thomas, and Telatin (2001) and Raffer (2001).

more creditor accountability, more donor generosity, and more emphasis on participation by the poor and civil society groups.

We ourselves partly agree with both points of view. We would combine their perspectives, summarizing the failure of past assistance programs manifest in the HIPCs' unsustainable debt in three broad categories (our proposals below for additional relief and a new aid architecture respond to this assessment):

- First, and probably most important in the short run, is a characteristic of many HIPCs associated with the poverty trap argument: their vulnerability to adverse, largely unpredictable shocks. Commodity price shocks leading to deteriorations in the terms of trade are the quintessential case in point, but hurricanes and other climatic disasters, and civil conflicts sometimes imported from neighboring countries, have also afflicted them.

- Second, and probably most important in the long run, are the failures of leadership associated with the view that much foreign aid goes down the rathole. These sometimes contributed to civil conflict; they sometimes took the form of bad governance (from straight looting by the leadership to a failure to stand up to vested interests on behalf of the common good); and they sometimes involved misguided policy choices, from a resort to inflationary finance to the neglect of the social sectors.

- Third is bad lender behavior and the sometimes well-intentioned missteps of donors that both sets of critics point out: pushing exports embodying inappropriate technology by the offer of export credits, and pushing loans to satisfy lending targets even when recipient government programs were not credible and the projects to be financed were of dubious value.

Of course, all these factors interact. A well-governed country suffering repeated adverse shocks will seek to diversify its economy, but that does not happen where governance is weak. And a well-governed country will resist the lure of export credits unless the goods being offered are really needed, but that is a secondary consideration in a country where the decision makers are motivated by the chance of getting a cut of the proceeds. In these circumstances, debt escalates but the ability to service it does not.

No one is particularly satisfied with the changes introduced through the 1999 enhanced HIPC Initiative. For the first set of critics worried about a foreign aid rathole, the enhanced initiative retains some traditional conditionality. The IMF must still give the nod that macroeconomic policies are adequate for a country to reach the first step in the process, the decision point. But the changes do not address the deeper concern about poor governance and overeager donors. They reflect increased political pressure to deepen and speed debt relief, and may actually make it easier for debtor countries to continue wasting resources and for donors to avoid the tough decisions more discipline would entail.

The changes respond more directly to the second set of critics calling for more debt relief and more aid to help countries escape poverty traps. The enhanced HIPC Initiative is bigger (more costly for donors) and faster—countries can reach the completion point within months instead of as long as 9 years. It also embodies an important change in the philosophy of conditionality by requiring demonstrated participation by the population in formulating the program to reduce poverty before debt-stock reduction is finalized. But for the second set of critics, the changes are still too small, too onerous for debtor countries, and leave too much control in the hands of official creditors, who bear considerable responsibility for creating the problem in the first place.

On the amount of debt relief, the second set of critics has raised three technical issues, which we now explore. The first issue is that the key criterion for identifying the countries that are eligible for debt relief, and which in most cases determines the extent of relief to which they are entitled, is inappropriate (Eurodad 2001, 2000). As was explained above, that key criterion is the ratio of the NPV of the stock of debt to exports. The criticism is that this is not really germane to whether a debtor country can afford to divert resources away from key social expenditures to service outstanding debt. Limiting such diversions was proclaimed to be an underlying purpose of the HIPC Initiative: that is reflected in the conditionality attached to the initiative, which is designed to ensure that the freed resources are indeed used for social programs and for other investments most likely to reduce poverty.

It is quite possible for a country with a high export-GNP ratio to simultaneously have a moderate debt-export ratio and a high percentage of its tax revenue preempted for debt service, thus threatening its ability to provide adequate social services to its population. The enhanced HIPC Initiative acknowledged that this could create a problem, and provided that a country with a high export-GNP ratio could qualify for debt relief under an alternative criterion. If its tax revenue was at least 15 percent of GNP (a requirement intended to avoid countries getting debt relief without making a serious effort to address their own problems), then its debt stock could be reduced to 250 percent of fiscal revenue. Thus the enhanced initiative acknowledged the problem, but the solution it chose left countries with sharply differing burdens of debt service relative to GNP, as inspection of the final column of table 2.4 (for the countries to have reached decision points) reveals.

The European Network on Debt and Development (Eurodad) argues that the logical approach would be to calculate the maximum affordable level of debt service and use that to calculate what percentage of the debt stock needs to be canceled, rather than decide to cancel a part of the stock of debt based on a comparison with exports. Those who subscribe to this line of thought are prone to make comparisons showing that spending on debt service exceeds that on health in some HIPCs (Drop the Debt 2001; Pettifor, Thomas, and Telatin 2001).

Eurodad also argues that debt reduction should be tailored to the circumstances of each individual HIPC. They suggest a formula that takes government revenue (including grants) and compares it to a minimal level of essential expenditure, consisting of country-specific estimates of the social expenditure necessary to achieve targets for health, AIDS, education, water supply, and sanitation (Eurodad 2000). (Somewhat quixotically, spending on things like security and parliaments is labeled "inessential" and assumed to come out of the pool also legitimately available for debt service.) They propose that 30 percent of the excess of revenue after providing for this basic level of essential public expenditure on the social sectors should be devoted to debt service. In the case of 10 countries, there would be no excess at all, which leads Eurodad to advocate 100 percent debt cancellation in those cases. Other countries would have their debt reduced to the extent needed to cut debt service to an "affordable" level. Where even that did not suffice to finance the minimal package of social expenditures, Eurodad advocates additional grants.

Debt campaigners contend that the likely reason donors have not adopted that approach is that it would raise the cost above what is politically acceptable. They believe that the scope of the HIPC Initiative and thus the guidelines used to define the initiative (e.g., the debt-export ratio vs. the development needs of the poorest countries) have been constrained by the political limits to the creditors' willingness to pay. And indeed, even the enhanced initiative is not fully financed, in the sense that the HIPC Trust Fund will require additional donor contributions if the multilateral development banks are to continue to be reimbursed for the cost of the HIPC Initiative after 2005. Some debt campaigners (Drop the Debt 2001; Oxfam 2001) and Roodman (2001) oppose the attempt to insulate multilateral development banks in the first place. They argue that the World Bank and IMF could afford to cancel all the debts owed to them by the HIPCs without threatening their financial integrity. Drop the Debt (2001) retained an accounting firm (Chantrey Vellacott) to investigate whether the World Bank's triple-A credit rating would be threatened if it drew on its capital to cancel HIPC debt; it concluded that the rating would be safe.

Moreover, a related argument is that forgiving unpayable debts is simply accepting reality, not doing debtors a favor (Roodman 2001). Cohen (2000) has used a model estimated on data from the Latin American debtor countries to infer what the market value of HIPC debt would have been in the absence of a willingness by the donors to extend new finance to enable debt service to be paid. He concludes that on average a reduction of the debt-export ratio from 250 to 150 percent was worth only about a tenth of the nominal write-down. That implies that about 90 percent of the debt reduction ought to be counted as a loss (bad debt), and only the remaining 10 percent as ODA.[24] Other comparisons suggest a figure in the same ballpark. For example, in the 1980s the commercial bank debt of Bolivia (now a HIPC) was quoted at under 10 cents on the dollar before the Brady Plan. And the US government, which is mandated by Congress to estimate the present value of its loan portfolio and expense reductions in value as they occur, applies a 92 percent discount to its HIPC debt (GAO 2000).

These calculations imply that deeper debt relief, to the point where it accepts the reality of what the debt is really worth, would not actually cost donors much. (It is true that at last count about 85 percent of the debt service due was still being paid, but the reconciliation between these figures is to be found in the tendency we have already noted for donors to direct new disbursements to countries that would otherwise encounter difficulty in servicing their debt. Defensive lending can be considered a form of de facto debt reduction.)

The second issue is that, even if the debt-export ratio were to be accepted as the appropriate criterion for calculating the extent of debt relief, the 150 percent benchmark is dubious. Pettifor, Thomas, and Telatin (2001) argue that this figure is essentially arbitrary, being based on no more than a rule of thumb. Eurodad (2001) concedes that the rule of thumb is based on a certain empirical regularity: the finding that defaults become much more common when debt-export ratios exceed something like 200 percent. But, it argues, that empirical regularity is based on the experience of a different group of countries, most of which were much richer than the HIPCs, and therefore found it less difficult to mobilize the resources needed to service debt.

The third issue relates to the debt sustainability analyses that the World Bank-IMF team has been conducting to decide whether HIPC debt relief is enough to make the countries' debt burdens sustainable (Eurodad 2001; Pettifor, Thomas, and Telatin 2001; Culpeper and Serieux 2001). These are projection exercises, designed to test whether the proposed debt reductions are large enough to enable countries to keep their debt-export ratios below 150 percent in the longer term (interpreted as out to the year 2017).

---

24. Most of the debt campaigners' literature does not recognize this discrepancy. Cohen's analysis also illustrates the fact that a write-down increases the value of the remaining debt. E.g., were they provided the opportunity in a commercial market to reduce their total debt stock from 150 to 100 percent of exports by buying it back themselves, the estimated discount (based on the Latin American data) would be 70 percent rather than 90 percent.

Figure 2.6 Realized and projected annual growth rates, 1980-2015

percent per year

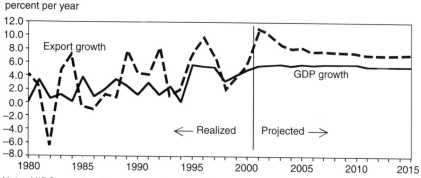

Note: HIPC growth rates are calculated as simple averages of World Bank DSA data.

Source: World Bank, *Global Development Finance* CD-ROM, 2001, and HIPC Debt Sustainability Analysis (DSA) documents.

To undertake such projections, it is of course necessary to project a path for exports (as well as new borrowing). The forecast is that on average the growth of exports in nominal terms of the 22 HIPCs that had already reached decision point in early 2001 will accelerate from 4.6 percent a year in the 1990s to 8.6 percent a year during the present decade (World Bank and IMF 2001a, table 7). A major reason for this improvement is that their terms of trade are forecast to improve at 0.5 percent a year, instead of deteriorating at 0.7 percent a year as they have in the past decade. The main criticism is that these export projections are too optimistic; though some recovery in their terms of trade is not impossible, the secular tendency for more than a century has been for some deterioration. Figure 2.6 displays just how much better the projected performance is than the historical performance has been.

Not only are the central forecasts asserted to be on the optimistic side, but critics note that these countries have historically been subjected to severe shocks, for which the analysis makes no allowance (Pettifor, Thomas, and Telatin 2001; Oxfam 2001; Culpeper and Serieux 2001). This again is illustrated in figure 2.6. There is no question but that the assertion is correct, but of course it is difficult to build shocks into projection models, because shocks are by definition unforecastable.

Clearly, it is important that *policy* should allow for the likelihood that countries will periodically be subjected to shocks, even if shocks cannot sensibly be incorporated into a projection model. Indeed, the World Bank and IMF could counter that a purpose of reducing the debt-export benchmark from 200 to 150 percent was precisely so that likely shocks would not push countries straight back into unsustainable territory above 200 percent. They also announced in August 2001 a procedure whereby a new debt sustainability analysis would be conducted at the completion point (World Bank and IMF 2001b). Any country that was established to have suffered a severe exogenous deterioration in its circumstances after decision point that threatened to jeopardize its debt sustainability might be entitled to additional relief at completion point, beyond what was promised at decision point.

Oxfam (2001) criticizes the projections of economic growth, rather than of export growth, as also being implausibly optimistic (again, see figure 2.6). In particular, it argues that the forecasts of growth for the African countries have failed to factor in the devastating effects of the HIV/AIDS epidemic on future growth. This might not affect the debt-export ratio, but it would matter in two other key ways. First, it would imply a lower rise—or no rise at all—in living standards over time. Second, it undermines the plausibility of the benign scenarios of a declining level of debt service as a share of government revenue that were presented in World Bank and IMF (2001a, table 7).

We said that this chapter would provide background about, and present the principal critiques of, the current HIPC Initiative. We have summarized our assessment of how the HIPC debt problem occurred in the first place, and we have described the many issues raised by various critics of the initiative as fairly as we can. We turn now to offering our own judgment on which of these critiques makes sense and on what sorts of actions should be adopted in response.

3

The Case for More

We argue in this chapter that there is indeed a compelling case for the donor community to do more than is currently envisaged to help the HIPCs. This case is based on two internationally agreed-on objectives, both of which we also regard as appropriate, and thus as constituting a sensible and hopefully uncontroversial basis on which to judge how much is enough.

The first is proclaimed as the official objective of the HIPC Initiative: "The principal objective of the Debt Initiative for the HIPCs is to bring the country's debt burden to sustainable levels ... so as to ensure that adjustment and reform efforts are not put at risk by continued high debt and debt service burdens."[1] The second relates to what is really the underlying objective of the HIPC Initiative, which we identified in the preceding chapter: the promotion of poverty alleviation and human development. The international community has officially endorsed a set of Millennium Development Goals for the year 2015 that quantify its agreed-on aims in this regard. Initially proposed (as International Development Goals) by the Organization for Economic Cooperation and Development (OECD) Development Assistance Committee (DAC) in 1996, these goals were reshaped in an agreement with developing countries and endorsed by the UN Millennium Summit of Heads of State in September 2000.

Debt Sustainability

We first consider whether the enhanced HIPC Initiative reduces these countries' debts sufficiently to make them sustainable. The World Bank

---

1. See http://www.worldbank.org/hipc.

and IMF (2001a) presented a study to the World Bank-IMF Development Committee in April 2001 that was intended to establish whether the enhanced HIPC program had reduced the countries' debt burden enough to make their debt sustainable in the longer term. According to that study:

> A country can be said to achieve external debt sustainability if it can meet its current and future external debt service obligations in full, without recourse to debt reschedulings or the accumulation of arrears and without compromising growth. (World Bank and IMF 2001a, 4)

Rather than attempt any direct estimation of the point at which debt service obligations begin to jeopardize growth, the study drew on a historical analysis to argue that countries have usually serviced their debts on schedule as long as the ratio of the present value of debt to exports was less than 200 percent. This figure was in fact embodied in the original HIPC Initiative as the standard to which debts should be reduced. The enhanced HIPC Initiative reduced this figure to 150 percent, so as to give some headroom for debts to rise again without quickly throwing countries back into debt service difficulties. The study built projections intended to illuminate whether the HIPCs could expect to maintain the ratio of the NPV of their debt to exports below 150 percent to 200 percent during the next 20 years.

The World Bank and IMF (2001a, appendix table 3b) study offers projections for the debt-export ratio for each of the 22 HIPCs that had already reached decision point by the end of 2000 out to the year 2017. For 9 of the 22 countries, projected debt-export ratios are less than 150 percent throughout the period. For another 4, they edge over 150 percent only for a single year. At the other extreme, Bolivia remains in the 150-170 percent range throughout the period, and 6 countries remain over 150 percent for more than 5 years. All countries except Bolivia are projected to be trending down in the later part of the period.[2]

As was noted in the previous chapter, these projections have already attracted a lot of criticism. It is therefore important to assess how much credence should be placed in them. Projection exercises are inherently fragile, and so it is important to ask whether the assumptions are conservative ones, or whether there is a lot of scope for worse outcomes. And how sensitive are the conclusions to reasonable variations in the key assumptions?

The variables of central importance in judging the realism of these projections are the real growth rate of exports; the terms of trade; and the growth, composition (i.e., mix of grants and loans), and terms of new

---

2. Because Bolivia is one of the two middle-income HIPCs, it may be that it is capable of carrying a heavier debt load than most other countries covered by the initiative.

external financing.[3] The average real annual growth rate of exports is projected to accelerate from 4.6 percent in the 1990s to 8.6 percent in the present decade (this is the unweighted average for the 22 countries given in the study's table 5). An average annual terms-of-trade decline of 0.7 percent in the 1990s is projected to give way to an improvement of 0.5 percent. New borrowing is projected to decline from an annual average of 9.5 percent of GDP in the 1990s to only 5.5 percent in the current decade, presumably with the loss made good by an increase in grants. The grant element in new borrowing is projected to almost double, from 30 to 58 percent.

One can certainly hope that policy improvements will have the effect of accelerating the growth of exports and GDP, though the projected increases (especially that of GDP from 3.0 to 5.5 percent) are substantial. It is not unreasonable to hope that the severe decline in the terms of trade these countries experienced in recent years will be reversed. One indeed hopes that the donors will replace loans by grants and ease the terms on those loans that remain. But these cannot reasonably be described as central assumptions, let alone conservative ones. They are what one can hope will happen under favorable conditions, rather than what one can have confidence will materialize.[4]

Are the projections sensitive to these outcomes being materially worse than assumed? Unfortunately, the answer appears to be yes. The World Bank-IMF paper tells us that "during the Board discussions of the first 22 HIPCs to reach decision points, concerns were raised that small deviations from the . . . projections could jeopardize debt sustainability" (2001b, 22).

This is illustrated by figure 3.1 (figure 3 of the World Bank-IMF paper), which shows the projected path of the average debt-export ratio declining monotonically from the year 2000 on. It also shows a "lower case sensitivity analysis" in which the ratio declines less rapidly, and a projection showing what would happen if exports grow at the same rate as in the 1990s. In the last case, the debt-export ratio rises monotonically (though it is still on average somewhat below 200 percent in 2017), almost as fast as it falls under their base case. One may infer that the HIPCs will need an acceleration of export growth of close to 2 percent a year to achieve declining debt-export ratio. Even if the average country achieves this, the

---

3. The assumption in all the HIPC exercises that savings on debt service are translated into increases in government spending implies that the gross new inflows of foreign resources remain unchanged (as is pointed out in a report of the US General Accounting Office; GAO 2000).

4. It is not clear that the IMF-World Bank team that drew up the debt sustainability paper would disagree. They write: "Raising the average annual growth rate by 2-3 percentage points (as projected in the scenarios underlying the debt sustainability analyses) should be feasible by strengthening the economic reform agenda and forging greater social cohesion . . . that could be unlocked by the PRSP process." (World Bank and IMF, 2001b)

Figure 3.1 Ratio of NPV of debt-to-exports for HIPCs at the decision point, projections, and past export trends

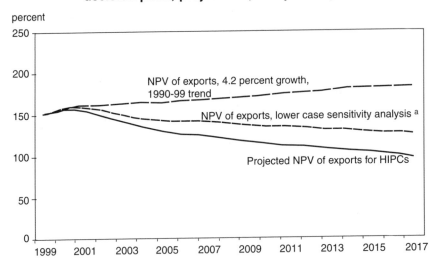

percent

NPV of exports, 4.2 percent growth, 1990-99 trend

NPV of exports, lower case sensitivity analysis [a]

Projected NPV of exports for HIPCs

a. Effect of 1 percent lower export growth, based on sensitivity analyses from decision-point documents.

Note: Excludes countries that qualified under the fiscal openness criteria.

Source: The Challenge of Maintaining Long-Term External Debt Sustainability, progress report by the World Bank and the IMF, 20 April 2001.

vulnerability of these countries to shocks makes it highly likely that some countries will fail to do so and will consequently run into renewed trouble.

The World Bank-IMF paper also reports a variety of downside scenarios concerning worse financing terms in half of the 22 HIPCs that had reached decision point. Although the effects of some of these scenarios in some countries were minimal, in others they were substantial. For example, if Benin received only half the level of grants that is assumed, then the ratio of the NPV of debt to exports would increase by 50 percent above the level projected.

It seems clear that the enhanced HIPC Initiative does not suffice to provide reasonable assurance that these countries will achieve debt sustainability as a result. Something more is needed. We will argue later that ensuring this objective requires a strategy specifically directed to ensuring sustainability even in the face of shocks.

The Millennium Development Goals

The Millennium Development Goals for 2015 are: to cut in half the proportion of people living in extreme poverty, of those who are hungry, and

Figure 3.2 "Group of Eight" by Dan Wasserman

of those who lack access of safe drinking water; to achieve universal primary education and gender equality in education; to accomplish a three-fourths decline in maternal mortality and a two-thirds decline in mortality among children under the age of 5 years; to halt and reverse the spread of HIV/AIDS and to provide special assistance to AIDS orphans; and to improve the lives of 100 million slum dwellers.

An earlier version of these goals differed slightly (e.g., by including universal access to reproductive health care and a reversal of the loss of environmental resources, and by excluding specific mention of AIDS orphans and slum dwellers). But a set of goals that includes halving poverty, achieving universal access to primary education, stemming the AIDS epidemic, and securing striking reductions in maternal and child mortality have been endorsed by the international community about as strongly as the international community has collectively ever endorsed anything.

As the cartoon (figure 3.2) suggests, setting goals is at best a meaningless act, and at worst hypocritical, without a willingness to follow through with measures that can be expected to achieve them. The unifying theme of the report of the UN High-Level Panel on Financing for Development (United Nations 2000, often referred to as the Zedillo Report[5]) is its attempt to elucidate what that would imply in terms of actions by both industrial and developing countries. The report described the types of actions by developing countries—in governance, macroeconomic discipline, public expenditure, financial-sector reform, and so on—that it believed were necessary if those countries were to generate the sort of equitable growth needed to achieve the goals. It emphasized that addressing their fundamentals along the lines identified was not merely a matter of political will but was going to demand a major focus on capacity building to strengthen many of their institutions.

The report also argued that these actions by developing countries should be regarded as a necessary but far from sufficient condition for achieving the goals. Complementary actions by industrial countries were going to be essential, in several dimensions. The industrial countries need to liberalize their imports of those goods that the developing countries are best placed to produce competitively. They need to maintain a liberal regime so far as capital exports are concerned, particularly with regard to foreign direct investment. And they need to provide a very substantially larger flow of aid than the current level of about $56 billion a year.

An attempt to quantify the additional flow of aid needed to complement country efforts to achieve the goals suggested an amount of about $50 billion a year, if all the poor countries were to qualify by virtue of their effort (see box 3.1). The subsequent deliberations of the Commission on Macroeconomics and Health, which quantified the need for additional health expenditure alone at $27 billion a year, suggests that the $50 billion estimate is probably conservative (WHO Commission 2001).

One of the studies on which the Zedillo Report drew in developing its estimate, Collier and Dollar (2000), concluded that even on present trends the overall target of halving world poverty may well be achieved because of the progress being made in Asia, where the bulk of the world's poor people still live. But it also concluded that the prospects in sub-Saharan Africa, where most of the HIPCs are located, were for only a modest decline in poverty, from 72 percent today to 64 percent in 2015, using a poverty line of $2 a day (on a purchasing power parity basis) in 1993 prices. It is widely accepted that the Millennium Development Goals should be interpreted as goals for at least the major regions, and preferably for individual countries, rather than just for the world as a whole. On that basis, Africa, and the HIPCs within it, are not on track to achieve the goals or even come close.

Excluding China and India, both of which are on track to achieve the Millennium Development Goals, the population of the low-income countries is about 1.3 billion. Almost half of these people live in HIPCs, which suggests that the cost of achieving the goals in the HIPCs might

---

5. One of the authors of the present study served as project director for that report.

Box 3.1 The annual cost of achieving the Millennium Development Goals

The Zedillo Report (United Nations 2001) included an annex that presented a back-of-the-envelope calculation of the cost of achieving the Millennium Development Goals. This basically consisted in assembling figures from other sources. For example, studies by the United Nations Conference on Trade and Development and the World Bank were used as the basis of the estimate that halving poverty would cost an extra $20 billion a year.

This estimate assumed that all the low-income countries themselves would adopt appropriate policies to make aid worthwhile. It was argued that halving poverty could also be expected to halve those in hunger, so no additional cost was added for that objective. The $9 billion figure for the cost of achieving universal primary education came from the United Nations Children's Fund. The HIV/AIDS figure came from the UN secretary-general. In several cases, the report failed to locate a reasonably convincing figure at all. The final annual figures presented (in billions of dollars) were as follows:

Halving poverty and hunger	20
Halving population without access to safe drinking water	0
Achieving universal primary education	9
Achieving gender equality in primary education	3
Achieving three-fourths decline in maternal mortality	No estimate
Achieving two-thirds decline in under-5 mortality	No estimate
Halting and reversing HIV/AIDS	7-10
Providing special assistance to AIDS orphans	No estimate
Improving lives of 100 million slum dwellers	4
Total (approximate)	**50**

It can be asked whether it is legitimate to sum these figures: For example, surely the least-cost way of halving poverty will involve improving education? That is indeed surely a source of overestimation. Conversely, several objectives were not quantified at all. New efforts since the Zedillo Report suggest the necessary amounts may be greater; the World Health Organization released a report in December 2001 that called for $27 billion a year for a Global Health Fund to combat HIV/AIDS, malaria, and tuberculosis. We use the $50 billion estimate as a conservative measure of the likely order of magnitude of the cost that will be involved if the world takes the goals seriously.

be half the global cost (the $50 billion of box 3.1). We therefore take $25 billion as our order-of-magnitude estimate of the annual cost of achieving the goals in the HIPCs.

That can be compared to the savings in debt service that have been generated by the enhanced HIPC Initiative: $1.2 billion a year as compared with the debt service that was being paid, and $2.4 billion a year as compared with the debt service that was falling due, for the first 24 HIPCs. Relief to these first 24 HIPCs represents 70 percent of total projected HIPC benefits;[6] if we scale this number up, the enhanced HIPC Initiative would

---

6. See "The Financial Impact of the HIPC Initiative," http://www.worldbank.org/hipc/Financial_Impact_-_December.pdf.

still save all 42 countries less than $4.2 billion a year. It can also be compared to the saving in debt service that would come from total cancellation of the debt, which would be about $8 billion a year (for the 42 countries). Finally, one should compare it to the net resource transfer into those countries as a result of new aid inflows minus debt service, which averaged $11.7 billion annually from 1995 to 1999.

In short, HIPC debt relief is far from sufficient to finance achievement of the Millennium Development Goals, and would still be far from sufficient even if it were to offer complete debt cancellation. Equally clearly, the HIPCs need all the resources that debt cancellation would bring them.

We conclude that—on both of the criteria that the international community has endorsed and that seem to be relevant in judging whether the HIPCs have now been given enough help—the answer is no. The next question is what should be done about it.

4

What Form of More?

Perhaps the biggest difference between Group A (the finance ministry types) and Group B (the civil society types) is how they react to a positive answer to the question discussed in the last chapter. Many in Group B tend to take it as axiomatic that a positive answer implies the desirability of more debt relief: How can one even think of forcing countries to service their debts when they cannot provide minimally adequate social services to their people?

Group A members are more wedded to the principle that debt contracts should be regarded as sacrosanct unless there are strong reasons for revising them, on the ground that the observance of debt contracts is the basic prerequisite for credit markets to function. They note that countries can be provided with the same balance of payments help in an alternative way that avoids rewriting debt contracts, namely, by providing more aid. Another relevant factor is the differing distributional effects that result from debt cancellation versus the provision of additional aid, which may argue for preferring additional new aid.

We take the view that it is wrong to assume automatically that one route is superior to the other. We see the force of the proposition that debt contracts should be regarded as sacrosanct, and that increased aid should therefore be preferred, ceteris paribus. But we also see several reasons why ceteris may not be paribus.

In this chapter, we explore the five considerations that we believe are relevant in choosing between more debt relief and more new aid. We start by examining *political resonance*: whether and why debt relief generates more political support than additional aid. This is one factor that may enable debt relief to generate *additionality*, meaning that it results in a bigger transfer of resources to developing countries than would otherwise occur.

To the extent that debt relief does not generate additionality, however, some developing countries must be paying the bill for the debt relief that is granted to others. It is important to have an understanding of these *distributional effects*, both to avoid inadvertently penalizing some countries and to minimize the danger that the debt relief may come at the expense of countries that could make better use of resources in tackling poverty.

There are also *efficiency* considerations involved: We argue that these may make debt relief worthwhile even if there is no additionality or redistribution. Finally, debt relief may have a benefit by allowing donor countries to exhibit greater *selectivity*: that is, to target their future aid with more discrimination (in the positive sense) across poor countries— to those countries most willing and able to use aid effectively for social and economic development.

All these considerations need to be factored into the design of a program to improve the HIPC Initiative itself, and to reform the development assistance architecture so as to avoid reconstituting another generation of unsustainable debt. Those are the tasks we address in the next chapter.

Political Resonance

One difference between debt relief and new aid that never occurred to Group A types is that the debt campaigners would succeed in tapping into a political nerve that they had more or less despaired of exploiting. Aid fatigue had come to be accepted as a political fact of life, nurtured both by the widespread perception that much aid fed corruption and by the empirical finding that the level of aid a country received had no effect on how fast it grew (Boone 1996).

We told ourselves that David Dollar and his associates (World Bank 1998; Burnside and Dollar 2000) have established that the reason for the "failure" of aid is that so much of it has been driven by commercial or strategic considerations rather than a concern to promote development. Their analysis implied that aid is still a worthy cause if it is directed toward countries that have a lot of poor people and that have the good policies and reasonably competent institutions to enable aid to be effective. But we had more or less written off the possibility of overcoming aid fatigue. And then along come the debt campaigners, who mobilize a substantial segment of what we had thought of as an apathetic public in the cause of debt relief. Why the difference?

At one level, we must admit that it is because the leaders of the debt relief campaign proved far more adept at public relations than the worthy Group A types whose idea of action is to sponsor a UN resolution calling for countries to give 0.7 percent of their GNP as aid. But that simply pushes the question back a stage. Why were the Group B types who sponsored the debt campaign motivated to push for debt relief instead of for an increase in the aid budget?

Three reasons spring to mind. One is that aid has got a bad name for the reasons alluded to above: because statistics seemed to show that it does not do any good in combating poverty and promoting development, and because of its association with corruption. Debt relief seems so far, at least, free of that baggage. Drop the Debt (2001, section 3) relates a number of anecdotes about how debt relief has released resources for increased social spending. Surely the World Bank or the Canadian International Development Agency could find some equally compelling stories about how their lending has supported better education and more health facilities, but these would probably be greeted by a cynicism that does not yet plague stories about debt relief.

Another reason is the biblical foundation of the Jubilee movement, which provided a simple, emotionally appealing rationale to wipe the debt slate clean. It was the religiously inspired nature of this movement that brought individuals like Pope John Paul II, Senator Spencer Bachus, and Pat Robertson to strongly support it. This factor was also influential in bringing out much grass roots support for the cause.

But we suspect there is a more fundamental reason. Though many of the most militant debt campaigners have implicitly called for unconditional aid, from its beginning the Jubilee movement itself called for linking debt relief to an entirely new approach to aid. It called for an end to the traditional use of economic conditionality in favor of the link to a poverty strategy "owned" by each country; that is, a link to greater social spending, more budget transparency, and greater openness to civil society and public participation in formulating and monitoring the use of resources "released" by debt relief. Debt campaigners in the United Kingdom and the rest of Europe took this position because their partner groups within debtor countries insisted on it, fearing that their own governments would otherwise waste or steal any new resources.[1] In the United States, debt campaigners supported the legislative efforts in Congress to link debt relief to poverty reduction.[2]

This concern that released resources should be used for legitimate purposes is the flip side of what we believe fueled the political momentum behind the debt campaign. This is the belief that the debts the HIPCs

---

1. Personal conversations, at the World Institute for Development Economics Research (WIDER) conference in Helsinki in August 2001, and with Ann Pettifor in October and November 2001.

2. The campaigners urged that third-party civil society groups rather than official donors, including the World Bank, have greater monitoring power.

were being asked to service were "unjust" or "illegitimate" debts, in the sense that they had not been incurred to promote the well-being of the populace of the countries in whose name they were taken on.

As was described in the last criticism of the HIPC Initiative at the end of chapter 2, much of the debt was incurred by dictatorial regimes that showed little concern for promoting the public good. Some of it was used to buy arms used to repress the population, some was promptly recycled in capital flight by the elite, and some was used to build white elephants rather than to make investments likely to generate growth. In the past three decades, as much as 60 percent of the value of all new debt commitments seems to have been made to countries that were subsequently ranked as "not free" or "corrupt" in international classifications (see appendix C for an elaboration of the figures). Many debt campaigners were clearly motivated by the injustice of requiring the mass of the population to undergo privation to service debts incurred for such dubious purposes, and this theme also resonated strongly with the larger public in both donor and debtor countries.[3]

A recent paper by Kremer and Jayachandran (2001) reminds us that there used to be a legal doctrine of odious debt, which argued that "debt incurred without the consent of the people and not for their benefit should not be transferable to successor governments." This doctrine was based on arguments advanced by none other than the US government. After the end of the Spanish-American War in 1898, the United States decided to repudiate the debt accumulated by Cuba under Spanish rule, and it developed this doctrine to justify its decision. The doctrine lingered on between the two world wars, but it has been forgotten in recent years. Even South Africa assumed the debts incurred by its former apartheid government, swayed by a concern that debt repudiation would be interpreted as a violation of the rules of capitalism that would jeopardize its standing in the international financial community and hence its possibilities for development.

But life is complicated, and there are good arguments against a sweeping use of the doctrine of odious debt. These arguments go beyond cynical creditor self-interest to the needs and interests of borrower countries and their citizens. Consider what effect the doctrine might have had on Indonesia during the long rule of Suharto, if its adoption had taken the form of allowing some quasi-judicial body to rule debts odious, and therefore uncollectible, ex post. Many people realized at the time that there was significant corruption in Suharto's Indonesia (although many

---

3. A group of Alabama church members brought to Washington by an NGO in 1998 talked about how wrong it would be to require people to choose between paying their debts and buying shoes for their children, and it was these individuals who were responsible for converting Republican Spencer Bachus into the champion for debt relief in the House (personal correspondence with Gerry Flood).

of us were surprised by revelations about its scale). Under the doctrine of odious debt, this would presumably have impeded Indonesian access to international loans, which were a significant support for Indonesia's impressive growth at the time.

Many people have forgotten it today, but acute poverty[4] in Indonesia fell from about 60 percent in 1970 to around 10 percent in 1996, possibly the fastest decline ever seen in a major country in all history. Unless one is quite sure that an inability to raise international loans on reasonable terms would have persuaded Suharto to mend his ways, or else that those loans were inessential to Indonesia's success, one might hesitate to endorse a policy that could have had the calamitous consequence of sabotaging the Indonesian miracle.

More generally, if unjust or odious debts were legally unenforceable, creditors and perhaps donors would soon recognize that they could not be sure debts that might be labeled odious would be honored in the future, and much lending that does do good would not take place. For example, lending that has, at least indirectly, supported strengthening of health and education systems would not go to countries with weak and unstable democracies (e.g., Côte d'Ivoire, Nigeria, Paraguay, and Peru), or to quasi-democratically elected leaders who have hung on to office for decades by less than democratic means (e.g., Egypt, Kenya, and Zimbabwe).

Even more perverse outcomes can be envisioned. Consider loans to Pakistan. No one could classify President Pervez Musharraf's regime as democratic. If Pakistan had been denied new loans when Musharraf first took office, he would have had no option but to suspend debt service. Would the donors then have retaliated against an action that they had effectively forced on Pakistan? If not, and they had let Pakistan "get away with it," the country would in effect have benefited from having acquired a government that was unambiguously undemocratic. That is hardly what advocates are hoping for.

In fact, Kremer and Jayachandran (2001) suggest that the doctrine of odious debt should be applied ex ante rather than ex post. That is, the quasi-judicial organ responsible would rule a regime odious, and from then on no debt incurred by that regime would be legally binding on a successor regime. That would mitigate the "Suharto problem" and the "Pakistan problem" identified above, but it would not resolve them. For if creditors feared that a regime such as that of Suharto—which for at least a decade was increasing the ability of its own people to effectively demand their political rights (as indeed they finally did)[5]—might be

4. Using the World Bank's "dollar-a-day" poverty line: $1 a day in 1985 prices, using purchasing power parity to convert from local currency into dollars.

5. Sen (1999) makes the point that political rights are intrinsic to and instrumental for economic development.

declared odious in the future, they would be quite rational in refusing to lend even in advance of such a declaration being issued, because the inability to raise new loans after the declaration would impede the servicing of loans signed before it.

Whatever the difficulties of legally codifying the doctrine, the fact remains that the sort of abuses that might justify considering debt to be odious provide a powerful political argument in favor of debt cancellation, one that may have helped to draw figures like the pope and Bono into the debt campaign. It is therefore worth examining how common it is to find the sort of grievances that make the case for declaring debt odious. We decided that the best way of getting some feel for that would be to examine a series of case histories. Appendix C therefore discusses five country case studies to give an idea of what proportion of the debt may have been incurred for dubious purposes. It examines the experiences of the Democratic Republic of Congo (the former Zaire), Kenya, Nicaragua, Pakistan, and Uganda (four HIPCs and one country that some people have argued ought to be a HIPC) during recent decades.

All the case studies exhibit instances that might justify the appellation odious for a part of the debt. To begin with, none of the five countries could claim to have been a democracy consistently during the past two decades. But even when they did have ostensibly democratic governments, as in Pakistan between 1988 and 1999, some of the rulers seemed more intent on furthering their family interests than on promoting the national welfare.[6]

Capital flight was significant in the Democratic Republic of Congo (where capital flight is roughly equal to the increase in the country's debt stock during the past two decades), Nicaragua in the late 1980s (22.4 percent of GDP between 1985 and 1998), and Uganda in the early 1980s. There was actually modest repatriation of capital into Pakistan and Uganda in the 1990s. Estimates of the personal fortunes amassed during their presidencies by Joseph Desire Mobutu in Zaire, Daniel Toroitich arap Moi in Kenya, and Anastasio Somoza in Nicaragua are striking—in each case, roughly half the size of their country's total outstanding debt at the time they left, or will leave, office.

Arms expenditures were a major factor in the Democratic Republic of Congo, in Nicaragua under the Sandinistas, and in Pakistan, although in Pakistan it is not clear that this was done in defiance of the wishes of the public. Although we were able to identify clear cases of spending on white elephants in four of the countries, they did not account for a large percentage of borrowing during the past two decades. In sum, though

---

6. One of the authors recalls a taxi ride in Washington the night before he entered the World Bank, inter alia to work on Pakistan. He happened to have a Pakistani taxi driver, who responded to a question about why he was so downbeat about the economic state of Pakistan: "They [meaning Benazir Bhutto and her cronies] are looting the country."

by no means can all the debts be considered odious according to all the criteria, it is not difficult to understand how history could be used to nurture popular indignation with forcing countries to service their debts.

Thus one can understand why a conviction that much of the debt was unjust, illegitimate, or odious may have contributed to political support for debt relief, while at the same time maintaining reservations about whether this principle could be applied in deciding exactly which debt, and thus what amount of total debt, to cancel.

Additionality

Debt campaigners assume that reducing debts will enable countries to spend less on debt service, and therefore more on other things, like education and health. Even at the level of the individual country, this proposition needs two qualifications. First, only the reduction of debt service that would have been paid releases resources; the reduction of debt service due that would have built up arrears just cleans up the books. Second, even a reduction of debt service that would have been paid results in increased resources only if other receipts, including aid receipts, remain constant.

Even if the aid inflow is unaffected for the individual country, might this come at the expense of a decrease in aid to other developing countries? We examine this latter possibility in the next section. In this section, we concentrate on asking whether there are reasons to expect that the grant of debt relief will lead to an increase in the total net flow of financial resources to all developing countries, which is what is meant by debt relief leading to additionality.

Assessment of the additionality (or not) of debt relief in the context of aid transfers faces two challenges. The first is that the underlying officially available data on grants, on the various kinds of subsidized loans, on interest payments—some paid, some reduced, some forgiven, and some owed but not paid—are difficult to unravel, particularly for individual debtor countries with many different lenders and donors. The accounting is perforce complicated. We discuss the issues in box 4.1.

At the end of the day, we judge the DAC accounting treatment to be appropriate, except in some relatively minor details. The way reduction of ODA debt increases measured ODA is not at the moment when the debt is forgiven but in the following years, when the country would have been due to repay the principal and does not have to. Because repayments of principal are counted as deductions from ODA, this means that a donor country that holds its disbursements constant in the future will register an increase in measured ODA.

The second challenge to measuring additionality is more fundamental and intractable, namely, that we can never know the counterfactual—

Box 4.1 Aid accounting and debt relief

The task of developing standard methods for counting aid is the responsibility of the Development Assistance Committee of the OECD. To qualify as official development assistance, a transaction must satisfy three criteria: it must emanate from the public sector in the donor country, it must have a minimum grant element of 25 percent, and it must have as its main objective the promotion of development in one or more relatively poor countries on an agreed list of recipients.[1]

ODA is measured net of principal repayments by borrowers on their ODA loans made in previous years. That is, borrowers' periodic repayments of principal (but not of interest[2]) are netted out of (and thus reduce) total transfers. The corollary is that when debt is forgiven, ODA in subsequent years is measured as higher than otherwise would have been the case by the amount of principal written off. This principle is correct.

When an ODA loan is forgiven, the donor reports the debt cancellation, but with an offsetting entry for a notional repayment of principal, which means that ODA does not increase in the year the debt is canceled. That also is appropriate treatment. Debt forgiveness is recorded, but does not add to ODA in the short run.

Are these procedures appropriate if the debt cancellation is not so much a voluntary act intended to benefit the debtor as an accounting recognition that the debt is uncollectible? Cohen (2000) argues that debt cancellation should be divided into two parts: the 90 percent (or whatever) that is uncollectible should be recorded as a loss on a bad loan, and the remainder should be recorded as debt forgiveness. That would make the uncollectible portion transparent, and it might create more healthy bureaucratic incentives for official creditors and guarantors to weigh carefully the risks that the loans they make may go bad, but it would not change the bottom line.

What about the flow accounts? The practice there is simply not to deduct from ODA repayments of principal that are not made. Certainly the contrary practice, to *deduct* repayments that are *not* made, would be nonsense! In principle, the right answer would be to count prior defensive lending as de facto debt relief that never built up a liability to be repaid. But after the fact, that is an analytic not an accounting exercise!

Where the conventional approach on the flow accounts does seem to give wrong answers is in relation to two second-order issues. The first concerns interest arrears. When ODA debt is canceled, interest arrears are canceled as well and are recorded—as an addition to ODA. Given that interest arrears are normally not paid because countries are unable to pay them, this is inconsistent with the principle that forgiving uncollectible debt is simply recognizing reality.

The second issue concerns the treatment of other forms of debt cancellation, of which the important one is cancellation of export credits extended to eligible countries. The DAC permits donor countries to count this as ODA, even if those loans would not have been serviced in the absence of debt forgiveness. This means that a donor country that holds its measured ODA constant when it forgives export credits that would not have been serviced in the absence of debt relief will actually be providing *fewer* financial resources than it would have done in the absence of debt relief. Additionality would actually be negative!

---

1. See http://www.oecd.org/dac/htm/dacdir.htm.

2. Had interest payments also been deducted from ODA, as is done in measuring resource transfer, and had loans all been serviced on the original terms, measured ODA might have become negative.

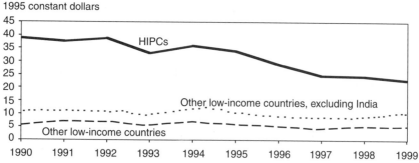

Figure 4.1 Aid to low-income countries in per capita terms, 1990-99

1995 constant dollars

Note: Figures are population-weighted averages.

Source: World Bank, *World Development Indicators*, 2001.

what would have happened in the absence of debt relief. We can only compare future aid flows with debt relief to past aid flows without the same relief.

The donor countries have pledged that debt relief provided under the enhanced HIPC Initiative will be additional to the aid they are already giving.[7] But good intentions do not always translate into action, and increased aid appropriations often have to run the gauntlet of legislators facing competing domestic needs and anyway suspicious of foreign "give-aways." Is there any way of knowing whether the current and additional proposed debt relief under the enhanced initiative will in fact add to the total resources available to developing countries?

During the past 5 or 6 years, as debt relief programs have intensified, total ODA has been declining (see figure 2.1 and table 2.1). A cynic would note that that decline coincides with a period when the benefits of the earlier rounds of debt cancellation should have been showing up in increased ODA. Figure 4.1 compares the course of aid per capita during the 1990s in all low-income countries and in those countries that benefited from the HIPC Initiative. Until 1997, aid declined in a more or less parallel way in both groups of countries. Had the initiative been additional, one would have expected to see the HIPCs facing a slower decline, or even registering an increase, after countries began receiving HIPC assistance in 1997. In fact, it is the non-HIPCs that registered a small increase after 1997, whereas the decline continued in the HIPCs. Although this is hardly decisive, it does suggest that any positive effect there may have been was very muted.

Conversely, if we examine the recent parliamentary processes in some of the donor countries, we might find a measure of comfort. For example,

---

7. "G-7 Finance Ministers Report on the Debt Initiative," presented at the Cologne Economic Summit, 18-20 June 1999.

Senator Jesse Helms, in his final days as chairman of the Senate Foreign Affairs Committee, persuaded the committee to approve a $435 million appropriation for the HIPC Initiative, which was almost certainly an addition to the funds that Congress would otherwise have approved for development aid. And other countries have also pledged funds for the HIPC Trust Fund, as well as forgiven bilateral debts. Perhaps the visibility of the HIPC Initiative secured more additionality than in the past. Of course, new aid appropriations are not the same as disbursements, and there is no way of being sure of what would have happened in the absence of debt relief. But the enhanced HIPC Initiative does seem to be inducing some, if only modest, additionality in comparison with the earlier record.

This modest additionality has come in the context of donor governments' allocations for their own programs of bilateral debt relief. We doubt, however, that more debt relief by the World Bank would be additional. Most debt owed by the HIPCs is owed to IDA rather than the World Bank itself, but it has been argued that the Bank could nonetheless draw on its accumulated reserves to write off those loans. Indeed, Drop the Debt (2001) argued that the Bank could do this without reducing its lending or threatening its triple-A credit rating, and a reputable accounting firm (Chantrey Vellacott) concluded that the claim was justified.

Even if this is correct, however, that does not settle the question. Entities with a triple-A credit rating pay a premium over the US Treasury to borrow that ranges from a few basis points up to about 75 basis points. The World Bank has recently been paying a premium of about 8 basis points over the US Treasury when it borrows. There is no question but that the sharp reduction in the Bank's capital and in its future operating profits that would result from the proposal to forgive all IDA and World Bank debts would increase that premium; the only question is by how much. If it were to rise by 50 basis points, which is easily within the range consistent with maintenance of a triple-A rating, that would increase the Bank's borrowing cost by about $75 million in the first year and some $550 million a year in the new steady state. The Bank would either have to pass that on to its non-HIPC borrowers in higher loan interest rates or progressively curtail its operations.

In either event, it is non-HIPC developing countries that would pay. In the new steady state, for example, Mexico would pay about an extra $50 million a year if the World Bank chose to pass the cost on, and India would pay an extra $36 million a year (on the basis of their present borrowing levels). Additionality would be achieved for all developing countries only if the loss to the non-HIPCs was less than the gain to the HIPCs. The latter have been quantified by Drop the Debt (2001, 4) as $215 million a year for the first 22 countries and $353 million for all the HIPCs.

Because our figure of $550 million a year for the extra steady-state borrowing cost is merely illustrative, this comparison does not establish whether or not additionality is to be expected. However, additionality would materialize only if the World Bank was previously being irrationally conservative in holding more reserves than could be justified. Conversely, the losses could exceed the benefits if reserves were forced down far below the optimal level. Perhaps the Bank is being too conservative in its practices, but we doubt very much whether it is so far from the optimum as to permit anything like a full funding of debt relief from its reserves without harming the interests of other developing countries by more than the benefit to the HIPCs.[8]

The African Development Bank (AfDB) is even less able to write off the debts it is owed without undermining its financial position than is the World Bank. The cost of the HIPC Initiative (in NPV terms) represents 102 percent of the AfDB's reserves and loan loss provisions. Comparable figures are 23 percent for the World Bank, 13 percent for the Inter-American Development Bank, and 20 percent for the IMF. Financing the HIPC Initiative is even more problematic for some of the small subregional development banks (see box 4.2).

The IMF is in a different situation, because it still has substantial holdings of gold on its books that are valued at the old official price of SDR 35 per ounce (currently about $45), in comparison with the market price of about $290 per ounce. It mobilized some of its holdings to finance the enhanced HIPC Initiative. The obvious approach would have been to sell gold on the open market and then use enough of the proceeds to keep the balance sheet whole and the remainder to forgive HIPC debt. But this proposal encountered objections, on the ground that selling gold would depress the market price. This would of course have been a correct reflection of the fact that part of a sterile stockpile of gold would have been released for productive use, making the world better off. But both gold producers and gold bugs were distressed at the prospect of a lower gold price and succeeded in blocking it.

Hence, in the event, the IMF devised an elaborate procedure that enabled it to tap some of the profits without selling gold on the market.[9]

---

8. To the extent that the debt is uncollectible, the World Bank's real reserves have already declined; what is at stake is whether the donors or the borrowers (or neither) should recapitalize it.

9. "In December 1999, the Executive Board of the IMF authorized off-market transactions in gold of up to 14 million ounces to help finance IMF participation in the HIPC Initiative. Between December 1999 and April 2000, separate but closely linked transactions involving a total of 12.9 million ounces of gold were carried out between the IMF and two members (Brazil and Mexico) that had financial obligations falling due to the IMF. In the first step, the IMF sold gold to the member at the prevailing market price and the profits were placed in a special account and then invested for the benefit of the HIPC Initiative. In the second step, the IMF immediately accepted back, at the same market price, the same amount of gold from the member in settlement of that member's financial obligations falling due to the Fund. The net effect of these transactions was to leave the balance of the IMF's holdings of physical gold unchanged." See from http://www.imf.org/external/np/exr/facts/gold.htm.

Box 4.2   The Central American Bank for Economic Integration

The example of the Central American Bank for Economic Integration (CABEI) highlights the distributive challenges of offering debt relief to a limited number of countries. CABEI has been operating since 1960, and it is the second largest source of financing for the countries of Central America. In 1999, when the enhanced HIPC Initiative was announced, it became clear that it posed a significant problem for CABEI. Two of CABEI's five members (Honduras and Nicaragua) were eligible for relief. Under HIPC terms, the burden of debt relief imposed was equivalent to half of CABEI's net worth.

For CABEI to have financed this effort without help from the international community would have threatened its solvency. Furthermore, it would have involved a transfer of resources from some poor countries to others, negating the underlying rationale for the HIPC Initiative. Thus the leadership of CABEI appealed to the World Bank and the international community for assistance in covering their share of debt reduction in Honduras and Nicaragua. An agreement was reached with the G-7, European Union, World Bank, and IMF for more than half of CABEI's share to be paid out of the World Bank's HIPC Trust Fund. Nevertheless, CABEI committed significant resources of its own to the HIPC Initiative, becoming the first institution to grant debt relief to Honduras ($252 million) in April 2000 (it subsequently wrote off $435 million of Nicaragua's debt).

Looking to the future, CABEI is constrained in its ability to lend to Honduras and Nicaragua, because under the HIPC arrangement it is not permitted to lend to these countries on nonconcessional terms, and it has not traditionally had a fund with resources for concessional loans. CABEI has created a new Special Trust Fund for Social Transformation in Central America to finance loans on concessional terms, but this facility has received only $9 million in commitments.

The profit from the operation was invested in an interest-earning account, and the interest on that investment is used to provide debt relief to the HIPCs.

The 1999 operation to mobilize gold involved only 14 percent of the IMF's 103 million ounces of gold. Hence there is plenty of scope for further actions of the same type, or for variants such as simply selling gold on the market. At the current price, this would yield more than $20 billion if the whole of the IMF's undervalued gold were to be mobilized. The IMF thinks that holding a lot of undervalued gold "provides fundamental strength to [its] balance sheet" and "provides the IMF operational maneuverability."[10]

More specifically, the IMF argues that its gold holdings matter in allowing even conservative central bankers to treat quota increases as an asset swap rather than a donation, because they know that if necessary the IMF could sell some gold to keep its balance sheet whole if some of its loans to distressed debtors were to sour. Though the IMF does indeed lend

---

10. See http://www.imf.org/external/np/exr/facts/gold.htm.

to countries with major macroeconomic problems, its record in recovering debts on its own balance sheet (as opposed to that of the PRGF, which has a separate balance sheet) is sufficiently sound to make it perfectly sensible for its members to treat quota increases as asset swaps, with or without the IMF's extra "gold" security.[11]

However, one should recognize that a likely consequence of forgiving the $5.6 billion of the IMF's claims on the HIPCs is that this might jeopardize the future of the Poverty Reduction and Growth Facility, the IMF's special fund for highly concessional lending to the poorest countries that cannot afford to borrow on its regular terms. The major industrial countries that control the IMF would be likely to conclude that they would be inviting new claims for debt reduction in the future if they were to maintain the facility. If the PRGF were therefore closed, it would eliminate loans now running at about $700 million a year gross and $100-150 million net, of which about 75 percent are to the HIPCs.[12] That would leave precious little additionality, even for the HIPCs, and would reduce transfers to other developing countries.

A report published in 2000, to which both authors of this study were signatories (Overseas Development Council 2000), urged that the PRGF be transferred from the IMF to the World Bank. The logic was that the development issues to which the PRGF is supposed to be directed are primarily the responsibility of the World Bank rather than the IMF (see box 4.3). Now that the World Bank has established Poverty Reduction Support Credits as a parallel to the loans of the PRGF, also directed to enabling low-income countries to implement their Poverty Reduction Strategy Papers, the bureaucratic obstacles to such a transfer are even less than they were then.

The report envisaged transferring the PRGF's assets, including its outstanding loans, as well as its liabilities. This could be done after the IMF had used a part of its gold stock to write off some or all of the (uncollectible) outstanding debts of the HIPCs to the PRGF, in effect "recapitalizing" the PRGF and providing a PRGF dowry to the World Bank. One would then not need to worry about the IMF abolishing the PRGF, because it would no longer have a PRGF to abolish. Reduction of any portion of the outstanding debts to the IMF would then be unambiguously additional, and the amount of resources available for concessional credits (or grants) from the World Bank would be increased.

Redistribution

The logic of the preceding section is that any additionality provided to an individual country by the enhanced HIPC Initiative will come at the

---

11. Lerrick (2000) makes this point.

12. Estimates based on 5-year annual averages (1997-2001); $500 of the $630 million in PRGF lending in 2000 went to HIPCs (IMF *Annual Report*, appendix 2, table II.6).

Box 4.3   The IMF's future role in development

A task force commissioned by the Overseas Development Council (2000) recommended that the IMF's Poverty Reduction and Growth Facility be moved to the World Bank. It argued that the IMF had an important continuing role in the poorest countries in macroeconomic surveillance and policy discussions, but that these need not be based on continuous lending and the associated conditionality. IMF loans should be made available only when countries encountered crises. Then countries could borrow under the IMF's traditional standby facilities. The task force suggested that some PRGF funds (now drawn from the World Bank) should be used to subsidize the interest costs of otherwise conventional standby loans for very poor countries.

The task force concluded that it was inappropriate to have the IMF in charge of a facility whose fundamental purpose is to provide development finance, the provision of which should be conditioned on the adoption of policies that will promote development. It is perfectly true that development requires prudent macroeconomic policies that will minimize the danger of crises and provide a supportive environment for growth. But it is also true that development policy has many other dimensions. These include governance and institution building, social policies in such areas as health and education, the banking system and corporate governance, policies toward trade and competition and privatization, and rural and urban policy. Except for the financial sector, where both institutions are involved, these are all areas in which the World Bank rather than the IMF has a mandate to develop a measure of expertise. It accordingly was deemed logical to concentrate medium-term, noncrisis lending in the World Bank.

The task force did not wish to see such a concentration lead to a reduction in financial flows to low-income countries. Hence, it recommended that the Poverty Reduction and Growth Facility be transferred from the IMF to the World Bank, complete with its financial assets, rather than simply closed. It envisaged continuing cooperation between the World Bank and IMF after the transfer, so as to bring the IMF's expertise to bear in assessing the macroeconomic policies being pursued by countries wishing to borrow. But the loans would come from the World Bank, with the IMF providing inputs to the policy assessment, rather than vice versa.

expense of other developing countries unless it is financed by additional ODA or by the mobilization of IMF gold. Through what channels can this occur, who is likely to suffer, and what are the consequences likely to be in terms of the reduction in global poverty?

The easy channel to understand concerns the redirection of bilateral aid. If a donor keeps its ODA constant in the years following debt reduction, when it is receiving fewer repayments than it would have, then some countries must receive fewer grants or new loans. In principle, it is possible that the donor could concentrate its ODA reduction on the countries whose debt was forgiven, in such a way as to leave the financial position of each recipient unaffected.[13] But the presumption is that the

---

13. Except that the recipients of debt relief would benefit from lower interest payments, which are not counted as part of ODA.

countries which benefit from debt reduction will not see their ODA allocations cut equivalently, and they will therefore benefit more than from the interest payments they no longer have to make. That benefit will come at the expense of those developing countries that receive reduced ODA.

Can anything be said about the likely consequences of such a redistribution? Yes, inasmuch as one of the key characteristics of HIPCs is that they are poorer than most other developing countries. Thus there is a presumption—no more—that debt relief will tend to redistribute aid toward poorer countries. However, if aid is to be effective, it should be concentrated in countries with particularly good institutions and policies, and these are not only or necessarily the HIPCs. There may in fact be a trade-off between the two Burnside-Dollar criteria: aiding poor countries and aiding countries with effective institutions and good policies (see box 4.4). That would leave one agnostic as to the net effect on poverty of redistributing aid toward HIPCs.

Consider next the case in which debts are forgiven by the multilateral institutions. Let us take IDA first, because it is the most important creditor of the HIPCs. Drop the Debt (2001), Lerrick (2000), Oxfam (2001), and Roodman (2001) all argue that the World Bank should draw on its reserves to forgive HIPC debt owed to the Bank itself and to IDA. As was noted above, Drop the Debt argues that this would not involve the Bank sacrificing its triple-A credit rating, which may be true but is nonetheless misleading, in that one would still have to expect its borrowing costs to rise. This would make it more expensive to borrow from the Bank, so the burden would fall on such borrowers, which means primarily the middle-income developing countries but also relatively low-income countries such as China, India, and Indonesia. It would be possible to make this cost transitional by rebuilding the Bank's reserves over time, but that would imply either cutting back the Bank's lending or else adding further to the cost of borrowing.

In either event, it is the World Bank's regular borrowers who would pay. The idea that the World Bank (let alone any of the other development banks) sits on a heap of functionless cash in the way that the IMF sits on a pile of sterile gold is just wrong. Tapping the World Bank's reserves would not be a free lunch, or impose financial penalties on the president or staff of the Bank, but (except to the extent that the Bank may hold higher than optimal reserves) would be paid for by its borrowers. Debt campaigners concerned with the plight of the world's poor need to be aware of the risk that the United States and other Bank shareholders will succumb to the pressure to use the Bank's reserves, because it has no financial cost to them—leaving the middle-income and non-HIPC Initiative poor countries to pay the tab.

How would the World Bank Group adjust if IDA's HIPC assets were to be wiped out? For the partial write-off under the enhanced HIPC

Box 4.4   Aid does work—if . . .

It is not surprising that the effectiveness of aid depends on conditions in the recipient country—and that aid provided to incompetent or corrupt governments is unlikely to generate growth or reduce poverty. It is easy to specify when aid does not work (Zaire in the past), but awfully hard to specify when it does. What do we mean by the conditions of "good governance" and "good policy" under which aid seems most effective? And might not some aid, though less effective, still be better than no aid at all (in improving people's lives), even when government is mediocre and policy unreliable (the way many citizens of the United States and European countries might describe their own governments!)? After all, most countries that need aid fall into that middling category.

On the basis of statistical analysis across countries and over time, Burnside and Dollar (2000) report that foreign aid is effective (encourages more economic growth) only where fiscal deficits are small enough, inflation is low enough, and the trade regime is sufficiently "open." For countries that are just average on these characteristics, aid accomplishes nothing in terms of growth. They conclude that aid works only where "policy" is adequate (essentially assuming that these macroeconomic conditions reflect good policy). They also conclude that aid does not in itself influence policy for the good. So they argue for aid based on "selectivity" across countries—that is, donors should channel aid only to those select countries that are already behaving well, with "good enough" policies and adequate institutions.

Other analysts question Burnside and Dollar's findings, arguing that their statistical results are too fragile to warrant a dramatic switch to such selectivity by donors (Hansen and Tarp 2001). Different samples and variables produce different findings. Aid seems to have diminishing returns, for example, and taking that into account reduces the apparent relevance of policy. Aid tends to be highest (relative to their GDP) in the poorest countries—a good thing in itself, because aid is meant to reduce poverty—but those may also be the countries where aid is most likely to have diminishing returns, because absorptive capacity is limited.

Cross-country statistical analysis can raise questions more effectively than dispose of them. Better understanding of exactly what and how certain policies and institutions at the country level make aid more selective is likely to come in the end from understanding specific country cases. Meanwhile, there is evidence that policies in the poorest countries, including the HIPCs, were better on average in the 1990s than in the 1980s (Birdsall, Claessens, and Diwan 2001; Burnside and Dollar 2001). So selectivity in aid transfers would actively benefit more countries today than it would have a decade ago. In addition, multilateral institutions have consistently been more selective than bilateral donors, probably because they are less vulnerable to immediate political pressures, and through such mechanisms as the Consultative Group of donors, the entire aid process has become more multilateral (Birdsall, Claessens, and Diwan 2001).

Finally, of course, even where some aid does not instantly "produce" growth, it can improve people's lives directly, if it contributes to reducing infant deaths, helping children stay in school, empowering disenfranchised women, and building local community organizations. If these outcomes also eventually help generate growth, all the better.

Initiative, the approach incorporated in present plans is to draw on a trust fund, which is funded partially by donors and partially by contributions from World Bank profits (the latter already a slight tax on non-HIPC borrowers). But even now donor contributions to the trust fund are not adequate to fully finance the enhanced HIPC Initiative (the money now in the trust fund will last only until 2005), let alone full debt cancellation. If the Bank's reserves are in fact higher than optimal, then it should certainly contribute more of its profits and use less of them to accumulate reserves. But we doubt whether this could be more than a marginal additional contribution. It would therefore be necessary to employ one of the three alternative approaches that have been suggested:

- Raise charges to the World Bank's regular borrowers (above the marginal increases that already reflect periodic contributions from the World Bank's profits to IDA and to the debt relief trust fund).

- Reduce future lending to IDA countries to match the reduced reflow of IDA funds.

- Invest World Bank funds in income-earning assets and use the interest earned to make grants to poor countries (Meltzer Commission 2000; Lerrick 2000).

We have already analyzed how the first approach would impose the burden on the Bank's regular borrowers, except to the extent that the Bank may currently be holding higher than optimal reserves.[14]

The second approach requires that other IDA borrowers bear the cost of forgiving HIPC debts. It is true that the fall in lending would be exactly equal to the reduction in amortization payments due from the HIPCs, so that there would be no collective benefit or cost to IDA's clients.[15] But though there would be no cost to IDA borrowers taken collectively, one again needs to ask whether there would be distributional effects. Perhaps the Bank could arrange for its IDA lending to each borrowing country to contract by the amount of the country's reduced repayment obligations, although one may suspect that this would provoke furious criticism that it was deliberately denying countries the benefits of debt relief.[16] Other-

---

14. The size of reserves is set according to policies periodically reviewed by the member governments, and is intended to optimize the trade-off between financial risk to the World Bank and borrowers' costs.

15. The reduction in amortization payments seems to have been overlooked by World Bank spokespersons, who have sometimes argued that IDA's inability to maintain the same level of new lending would be damaging collectively to the countries that borrow from IDA.

16. One could expect many more comments like these: "In an almost cynical game of bait and switch, countries like Mozambique have seen the benefits of debt relief canceled out by corresponding reductions in aid, resulting in no net gain for social development activities in the national budget" (Edmund Cain, "Helping Poor Nations Lift All Boats," *Atlanta Constitution*, 23 August 2001).

wise, the presumption has to be that loans to non-HIPC IDA borrowers would contract, so that they would be the ones paying for HIPC! That means IDA-only borrowers like Bangladesh and blend borrowers like India and Indonesia. Given that IDA has based its lending quite consciously on the Burnside-Dollar criteria, there is a strong likelihood that such a redistribution would have a perverse effect on the global fight against poverty.

The Meltzer-Lerrick plan is to have reflows into IDA invested in income-earning assets, and then use the income generated to make grants. The disadvantage of this is that, unless IDA reflows were to be supplemented by large additional donor contributions, the initial effect would be a severe reduction in the flow of IDA money. (If the assets in which IDA invested yielded 7 percent, then the flow would initially decline by 93 percent in the absence of additional donor funding.) The issues with respect to the regional development banks are similar, but more acute (remember box 4.2 on CABEI).

There are two morals to this discussion. The first is that additionality matters. The second is that it is wrong to think of the World Bank's reserves as a substitute for IMF gold or additional ODA in providing additionality. The Bank already uses any excess reserves to fund "worthy" purposes, of which the HIPC Initiative is only one. "Success" in raiding the Bank's reserves to forgive HIPC debt would come at the expense of other developing countries, perhaps ones that are equally poor and that have been making better headway in combating poverty. The result could well be a reduction rather than an increase in the rate at which global poverty declines and a further threat to achievement of the Millennium Development Goals.

Efficiency

Suppose that there were no additionality or redistribution whatsoever, but that other aid decreased just enough to offset debt relief and the reduction in interest payments, leaving each HIPC neither better nor worse off in terms of resource transfers. The HIPC Initiative might still be worthwhile, because for several reasons it might increase the efficiency of aid, meaning its effectiveness in generating development per dollar transferred. In this section, we trace five mechanisms by which debt relief might be expected to increase aid efficiency: ownership, reduced transaction costs, project-based aid, tied aid, and effects on private investment.

Ownership

In recent years, aid donors have begun to emphasize the need for recipient countries to take charge of the design of development strategy, to be "in

Figure 4.2 The increasing aid coordination challenge

number of donors

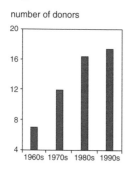

number of recipient countries

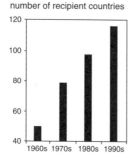

Theil index[a]

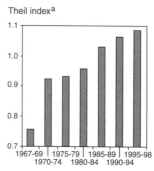

a. The Theil index is a statistical measure of the extent of concentration of aid by sector. Higher values of the index indicate that aid is spread over a greater number of sectors.

Source: World Bank, *Global Development Finance*, 2001.

the driver's seat," to "own" their development programs and priorities, rather than these being largely dependent on and set by donor decisions about development assistance. The fact is, of course, that the poorer a country and the more dependent it is on external funds, the larger and more complicated its task and the less likely it is to have the administrative capacity and the political wherewithal to cope. Country size is also a factor. China and India are much better able to manage the donor process, despite their low per capita income, than are small, somewhat richer countries like Congo and Honduras.

However, these well-meaning efforts are flying in the face of a basic trend during the past two decades—which for the HIPCs and most other low-income countries has been the reality of the donors' ever-increasing presence, measured both in terms of the number of donors and their annual inflows of new money. Behind the continuing if diminishing annual positive net transfers to most low-income countries, there has been a combination of gradual increases in gross transfers offset by gradual increases in debt service payments. The increases in gross transfers of donors and creditors meant that their involvement in the development programs of recipient countries was constantly increasing. Perhaps even more important, there has been a continuing increase in the number of donors operating in each country, and in the number of sectors over which each spreads its aid (see figure 4.2).

The increasing financial presence of donors reduces the space for governments to "own" their development programs. Government officials, constrained by high debt service obligations and by the need to keep the aid flowing, find their choices severely limited by donor preferences. To the extent that ownership matters, and the evidence is that it does (Collier and Dollar 2001), it would be much better to forgive the debt and cut new inflows. Even if there were no increase in net transfers, the country would regain the ability to decide for itself what it thought was worth doing, and governments would become more accountable to their citizens for consistent and coherent management of their own aid resources. In some objective sense, the decisions might be no better than those that result from present arrangements; but if they resulted in the government and public believing in what was being done, the end results could be expected to improve.

Reduced Transaction Costs

It is difficult to argue that the business of development assistance has in the past been conducted efficiently. The HIPCs and other low-income countries highly dependent on external assistance cope with dozens of donors and creditors, proposing hundreds of projects and programs, negotiating and monitoring elaborate and often different procurement and disbursement procedures as well as policy and program conditions. Donors make constant efforts to coordinate their activities, including through the Consultative Group process of annual meetings of all donors with officials of recipient countries, but that has not resolved the problem. In addition, until the beginning of the HIPC process, these meetings ran in parallel with repeated rounds of debt negotiations for most countries (see box 2.2 above).

Government officials of aid-dependent countries as a result often spend much of their time dealing with donors and managing within their own governments the interministerial and intergovernmental decisions about donor-financed programs. The World Bank alone might have half a dozen different missions visiting a country at the same time. In any week the minister of finance or of planning may expect to meet with some of these missions, as well as missions from the European Union, IMF, United Nations Development Program, United Nations Children's Fund (UNICEF), and several national aid ministries. They might discuss new financing, renegotiate existing programs, and consider reports on ongoing projects. In some cases, country officials would be coping with competing missions—from the World Bank and the Dutch with different approaches to agriculture, or from UNICEF and the European Union with different approaches to health or childcare.

Country officials might also, at least implicitly, have to adjudicate between the conflicting priorities of different donors and creditors, for example, between IMF demands for reduced government spending and World Bank pressures to sustain the government's prior commitment to an ongoing road maintenance program. The recent explosion of NGO-based aid, though still modest in volume, is highly management intensive, and adds further to the burden for governments.

A second benefit of a transfer-neutral reduction in debt is that it would reduce these transaction costs of obtaining aid. At present, one of the principal tasks of some government officials is to keep the donors happy and the aid flowing—aid that is then recycled back to the donors. It would free up the time of key personnel in the main economic ministries to focus on longer-term issues if they could be relieved of this task.

Project-Based Aid

Donors display a strong preference for supporting predefined discrete projects that they can describe to their taxpayers' representatives and claim credit for with the public of the recipient country. This is especially true of bilateral donors, who have been the largest providers of aid to HIPCs and sub-Saharan African countries in the past two decades. Thus most of their support has come in the form of "projects" as opposed to more fungible policy-based budget support or debt relief. The World Bank and African Development Bank also provide the bulk of their support in the form of projects, although multilaterals they are one step removed from the political pressures of donor-country legislatures, they are somewhat more able to provide program support.

Project support is relatively nonfungible, meaning that countries cannot easily shift resources earmarked by donors for a specific health project to infrastructure investment or vice versa. Of course, to the extent that project support is earmarked for an activity that the recipient government would otherwise have funded itself, the project is indirectly supporting some other activity the government chooses. If a government manages the donors effectively, it can thus create the kind of fungibility that is potentially more consistent with sustained, coherent planning. We have here, however, a chicken-and-egg problem. The more a government depends on immediate support, the less easy it is for it to manage the donors and seize ownership of its program—even when each donor in principle strongly supports that ownership.

Table 4.1 shows a breakdown of bilateral donor assistance to the HIPCs during the past 20 years, by 5-year period, into project support, program support, technical assistance, debt relief, and a category including food, emergency, and unallocated aid. These data do not show much increase in the share of bilateral assistance going to nonproject budget support, even if one aggregates debt relief with program support. In the past few years, however, donors have made efforts to support broader programs through the budget—for example, to supplement the health-sector budget once an overall health plan has been agreed on with the recipient government, rather than supporting the construction of clinics or the purchase of hospital equipment. The available data make it difficult to distinguish these newer broader "projects" from traditional ones, and so the situation may be somewhat less dire than is suggested by the table.

Table 4.1 Project versus nonproject activity: Commitments of bilateral ODA to the HIPCs, 1973-99 (percent)

Commitment	1973-79	1980-84	1985-89	1990-94	1995-99
Total program	17	17	18	15	8
Total project	35	36	41	40	44
Technical cooperation grants	33	31	27	28	24
Debt relief	3	4	4	9	13
Food, emergency, and unallocated aid	12	12	10	8	11
Total with food aid and technical cooperation	100	100	100	100	100

Note: Project aid includes the following sectors: social infrastructure and services, economic infrastructure and services, production sectors, and multisector.

Source: Organization for Economic Cooperation and Development, Development Assistance Committee creditor reporting system, *International Development Statistics* CD-ROM (various years).

In the absence of budget support, the governments' domestic budgets must finance debt service. In the case of HIPCs in 1999, gross disbursements from bilateral and multilateral donors were about $15 billion, of which not more than $3 billion was clearly in the form of general budget support.[17] Debt service paid from the budget was slightly more than $5 billion. Thus HIPC governments were financing a net negative transfer from their budgets of about $2 billion, despite receiving a large positive resource transfer.

Of course, if all the projects financed were in fact a high priority for the governments, there would be no harm done. The problem arises if the projects in fact reflect donor priorities more than country priorities. This is the case not only among investment options (health vs. roads) but also between spending on new investments versus spending to operate and maintain existing investments. Donors traditionally emphasize the importance of maintenance, but in fact they find it easier to finance new construction, which tends to reinforce rather than counter the incentives operating in countries where corruption is rampant. Building new preschool classrooms is more visible and more politically attractive than keeping schools in decent condition—not only for officials who manage to take a cut of new construction, but also for donors reporting to their legislatures on their development assistance programs.

In sub-Saharan Africa, the donors' involvement in new investments has been so great that the bulk of all public investment has been externally financed. Perhaps reflecting this dominance of donors in public invest-

---

17. By general budget support, we mean the $1.1 billion in bilateral budget support reported in table 4.1 and the $1.7 billion in IMF loans and World Bank structural and sectoral adjustment loans to HIPCs in 1999.

ment projects, public investment as a share of total investment is higher in Africa than in other developing regions, given income. Public investment is also high relative to the central government budget (one third and more) and to GDP, at 5 to 10 percent (World Bank 2000b). If the marginal return to public investment is low (Devarajan, Swaroop, and Zou 1996)—as appears to be the case in many countries in Africa, given their low growth despite substantial investment rates—a shift of resources from investment to budget support would probably generate higher overall development effectiveness.

Tied Aid

Aid is said to be tied when the donor requires purchase of the goods or services used in the project from providers based in that donor country. Collectively, donors have made efforts to reduce the tying of aid, and they have recently pledged to end the practice.[18] Unfortunately, this pledge exempted the two areas where tying is most costly to recipient countries: food aid and technical assistance. Loans from multilateral institutions are untied—or at least are tied only to suppliers based in a country belonging to the lending bank, which is not very restrictive for World Bank loans but may have more of an effect for loans from regional development banks. Debt relief is by its nature untied.

According to conventional estimates, tying reduces the value of aid to the recipient by 15 to 30 percent (Chinnock 1998). Because about 30 percent of the $22 billion in annual bilateral assistance other than technical assistance has been tied, this means that donors were choosing to waste something like $2 billion a year on lending other than technical assistance. The waste is far greater in technical assistance, now running at about $13 billion a year. (Technical assistance refers to support for advice and training, usually by consultants, and to manning the project implementation units that are set up to oversee projects.) This is virtually all tied to the donors' own professionals, who are often 10 or 20 times as expensive as those who could be hired on the world market from other developing countries.

If we conservatively assume that the efficiency loss of tying is 50 percent in the case of technical assistance, then tying costs about $6.5 billion a year. That will remain even after the OECD countries have implemented their pledge to abolish tying. In addition, tying may cost 30 percent of the yearly $1 billion in food aid. Even after tying has been "abolished"

---

18. At the annual meeting of the OECD's Development Assistance Committee in April 2001, the 23 DAC countries agreed to end the longstanding practice of tying aid to procurement in the donor country. The decision was billed, alongside continuing rounds of bilateral debt relief, as a sign of the donor community's commitment to strengthening the effectiveness of aid and increasing countries' ownership of their reform programs. (Even now, however, US Agency for International Development consultants must fly on US carriers.)

per the DAC pledge, therefore, total waste will probably be more than $7 billion a year.[19]

Tying—in addition to lowering the real impact of aid on development—has a less easily measured cost in loss of control and ownership by aid recipients. Tied aid eliminates incentives to minimize costs by establishing efficient purchasing systems, by maintaining processes of competitive bidding, and so forth. It also constitutes a form of protection for firms based in donor countries that may throttle any potential local supply.

Effects on Private Investment

Krugman (1988) and Sachs (1990) argued in the context of Latin America that a debt overhang implied that a substantial part of the benefit of future exports would accrue to creditors, because more export receipts would enable the debtors to service their debt more fully. This expectation diminishes the incentive for private investors, who may fear that their profits will be heavily taxed so that government can pay its debt service. Others (Addison and Rahman 2001) argue that the general uncertainty created by a high debt stock discourages investment in tradables with high returns but long gestation periods (e.g., coffee for export or garment factories), in comparison with less risky quick-return nontradables such as retail sales and construction—or perhaps simply discourages private investment relative to consumption.

These arguments suggest that a sufficiently large and visible reduction in a country's debt will sharpen the incentive to invest in a way that new aid transfers will not. The question is whether such a mechanism is operating among the HIPCs, so that reducing their high debt might play some role in releasing them from a poverty trap.

For poorer countries receiving publicly sponsored development loans, other, more fundamental, constraints may be more important in discouraging private investment. But the question, in the end, is an empirical one, which several recent studies have addressed. Two papers presented to a recent conference in Helsinki found such an effect (Dijkstra and Hermes 2001; Were 2001), whereas a third identified a positive effect for debt relief but estimated that it was mainly the result of reducing debt service rather than debt stock (Serieux and Samy 2001). We conclude that debt relief is more likely than an equally large but highly uncertain flow of new aid to reassure private investors about a country's economic potential. In other words, an assured dollar of debt relief is probably more efficient in generating development than a promise of a dollar of new aid.

---

19. All figures are aggregates from the OECD DAC *Handbook*. One restriction in assessing the effects of tied aid in HIPCs is in the reporting, because tied aid statistics are only presented in the aggregate.

With all these potential advantages of debt relief over new aid, why have donors and creditors been reluctant to reduce debt? One reason may be a desire to avoid undermining the principle that debt contracts should be considered sacrosanct. Another may be their own political and bureaucratic constraints, such as pressures on bilateral donors to tie their aid, which is possible only with new lending or grants. But perhaps the major factor is donors' lack of confidence in the capacity and accountability of recipient governments. The poorer the country and the weaker its institutions, the more likely is it to need assistance and the less likely is it to be a good user of that assistance.

In contrast to assistance earmarked for specific projects and programs, debt reduction has the property of releasing resources that might be used for programs the donors would not endorse—a military buildup instead of education, to take the classic example. Even if it is possible to monitor an increase in social spending (a characteristic goal of HIPC programs), it is not easy to monitor changes in other uses of government revenues. In particular, it is not easy to know the counterfactual; for example, whether, in the absence of the debt reduction, a government might have increased its revenue effort—including raising money from those who, though capable of paying taxes, have heretofore managed to avoid them. Debt relief, and particularly a one-time large debt reduction, also has the disadvantage of releasing the creditworthiness constraint, opening the door for impatient (or badly managed or corrupt) governments to accumulate official debt all over again (Easterly 2001), unless the donors are much more disciplined and accountable than they were in the past.

That project aid is also at least partly fungible—to the extent it allows governments to divert their own resources from projects they would have financed anyway to activities donors might not endorse—has not traditionally worried the donor community. The thinking goes, apparently (and reasonably), that some projects appealing to donors are not priorities for recipient governments and would not have been financed without donor help. In addition, donors, including the World Bank and the other multilaterals, are less vulnerable to accusations of ineffectiveness in the case of projects. They are accountable to their own legislatures or boards in a fiduciary sense for the projects they finance, and they can report on project outcomes.[20] Accountability for the programs they may "indirectly"

---

20. E.g., the World Bank management reports regularly to its board on the effectiveness of its projects. Even special reports, such as the Wappenhans Report of 1992, focused on the Bank's performance in terms of projects, i.e., on the number of projects deemed satisfactory in terms of rates of return and staff judgments of "development effectiveness." The Bank's fundamental effectiveness in terms of the effects of its support on overall development is much more difficult to assess. Only in the past few years has the Bank undertaken systematic research on this larger question of effectiveness at the country level. The results of some of those studies are cited in box 4.4.

finance, and for the overall performance of the countries they assist, does not exist in the same bureaucratic sense, and indeed cannot be easily surmised given the difficulties of inference.

Even where there is confidence in a current government administration, donors face the constant risk of a future deterioration in governance. Again, the poorer and less capable a country, the greater is this risk. The World Bank and the other multilateral donors can build in conditions for new loans, but they cannot in the same way link debt relief to future actions of a recipient government. Government commitments to a process of privatization of state-owned banking monopolies, or elimination of onerous regulations on small business, or increases in the proportion of total spending going to social investments, can be linked to releases of loan tranches; that is not possible in the case of a one-time reduction of debt stock, as is foreseen at the completion point in the HIPC program. Even if the debt stock reduction is actually financed over time, the donor commitment is made up front, and some of the expected benefits of the one-time reduction (especially greater confidence in the private investment community, and more control and ownership of medium-term programs by the government) are associated with its being treated as completely irreversible.

For these reasons, official debt relief in the 1990s was always a negotiated process, in which the official creditors tried to lock in future commitments about the use of the "freed" resources. The HIPC and enhanced HIPC debt reduction programs continued this approach. There was a new emphasis on the need for debtor countries to take the lead (the "driver's seat") in developing their own programs of poverty reduction. Conversely, the fact that the strategy to be developed is for poverty reduction—and that there are clear guidelines for the kinds of information and programs such a strategy is likely to entail—certainly reflects donor interests and priorities. (This is not to say that these guidelines may not also reflect recipient government priorities as well, only to highlight that they do reflect donor priorities.)

The bottom line is that countries can benefit from debt relief, especially outright debt stock reduction, even if it is not additional at all, that is, even if it is financed completely by reducing future new transfers. In part, that is because the value of new transfers is overstated to the extent they are tied, or constrained to expenditure on projects that generate lower returns than are available elsewhere.

Less measurable but also important is that debt reduction compared with new aid involves reduced donor presence and greatly reduced transaction costs of receiving aid. By releasing the budget constraint that debt service represents on fully fungible tax revenues, it increases the ability of debtor governments to control their own destinies, at least with respect to government policies and programs. It thus enhances ownership and automatically puts recipient governments in the driver's seat—the very objectives of the new approach to development assistance the HIPC Initiative is meant to embody. Finally, there is the evidence that sufficiently large and certain debt reduction is likely to reassure private investors more than the promise of future new aid.

Conversely, from the point of view of donors and creditors, debt reduction undermines their ability to withhold resources in the future from governments they judge to have become wasteful or corrupt, or that renege on earlier policy or program commitments. (To the extent that the debt is uncollectible, this ability is overstated but apparently still comforting.) The efficiency advantage of debt relief will be captured only in countries that are able to exploit the greater flexibility and improved capacity to plan and manage. In countries where politics go bad or even well-meaning leaders are not backed up by functioning institutions, debt relief has no real advantage over donor-driven and -managed projects. This brings us to our next issue: country selectivity.

Country Selectivity

Following the work of Burnside and Dollar (2000), it is more and more accepted that the reason that aid did so little to stimulate development in the past is that it was often given to the wrong countries (though even on this point there is still some debate; see box 4.4). Too often, it was directed to strategic or commercial ends, to corrupt dictators and countries on the verge of civil conflict, rather than where it could do the most good to promote development and reduce poverty. Burnside and Dollar showed that aid "works," in the sense of being effective in reducing poverty, if two conditions are satisfied. First, it must be directed to countries that have a lot of poverty, which is hardly surprising. Second—and much more difficult—it must be directed to countries that have capable institutions and policies.[21]

By country selectivity, we mean the ability and willingness of donors to channel resources to recipient countries on the basis of these two criteria: need, and the ability to use funds effectively. These criteria of course can conflict: poor countries are usually those with weaker institutions, and often policies. No one claims to know exactly how to pick optimally when faced with a clash of that sort. Nevertheless, just focusing on these two criteria and keeping strategic and commercial considerations out of the decision-making process would be an excellent start.

One of the less-appreciated consequences of the debt buildup since the 1970s has been the erosion of donors' ability to follow this principle. At

21. In chapter 6, we outline this problem further and suggest some benchmarks that could guide country selectivity by donors (see also box 6.2).

first, the main accumulation was of bilateral debt. Because donors feared the consequences of stopping the flow of finance, they progressively forgave the debt owed to them through Paris Club arrangements, and they began shifting their aid from loans to grants. But the multilaterals did not have those options. If they were to maintain a positive net transfer, they had to lend ever more. In consequence, a growing portion of the debt of today's poorest countries became debt owed to the multilateral institutions. For the HIPC Initiative countries, 42 percent of all official debt was owed to the multilaterals by 1998 (World Bank 2001b).

The consequence was that multilateral lenders came to receive an increasing share of debt service paid by these countries, while providing a declining share of net transfers to them (figure 4.3). This became a problem not only for the multilaterals themselves, but for donor governments. Because multilaterals are the preferred creditors, bilateral donors were anxious to avoid any of the poor countries falling into arrears to multilaterals. Moreover, bilaterals' switch in the 1980s from loans to grants was a short-term solution, in that this reduced their need to service bilateral debt and thus indirectly helped finance countries' debt service to multilaterals. Indeed, for several countries, donors contributed to special country trust funds that financed debt service to the World Bank.[22]

However, donors began losing their ability to be selective toward borrowing countries with high multilateral debt and high servicing costs for that debt. Birdsall, Claessens, and Diwan (2001) show that, in a sample of African countries, donors and creditors generally provided more transfers to poorer countries that scored better on the World Bank's internal measure of country policy and institutional capacity. This is especially true for IDA and the IMF. However, this was not the case for a subgroup of countries with unusually high multilateral debt.[23] For that group, donors (with the important exception of IDA[24]) collectively appear to have channeled resources independent of country capability.

The results of this study thus suggest that donors are not only aiming at development, by channeling more resources to poorer countries, but are also engaged in what might be called "forced" lending to countries that have accumulated high levels of multilateral debt. Even as they successfully encouraged multilaterals to be selective—avoiding lending to countries

---

22. An example is IDA's "Fifth Dimension," which consisted of funds allocated to IDA recipients to cover interest payments due on their IBRD debts. Another is the Tanzanian Multilateral Debt Fund, which was supported by bilateral donors and used to help service Tanzania's debts to the multilaterals, thus allowing Tanzania to stay out of arrears and be eligible for the HIPC Initiative.

23. Unusually high multilateral debt was defined as above the median of the group's debt-GDP and multilateral-debt ratios. The study refers to net transfers, as it should.

24. The Country Policy and Institutional Assessment (CPIA) scores were designed to guide IDA lending, so the result is not too surprising—but is nonetheless gratifying.

Figure 4.3   Aid and debt, sub-Saharan Africa, 1977-87 and 1988-98

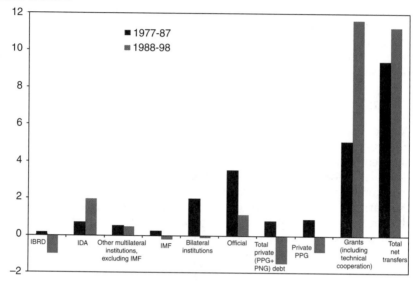

Annual net transfers to sub-Saharan Africa by category of creditors (in nominal terms)

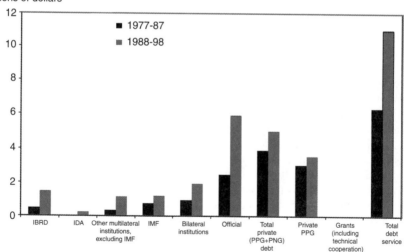

Annual debt service of sub-Saharan Africa by category of creditor

IBRD = International Bank for Reconstruction and Development
IDA = International Development Association
PNG = private, nonguaranteed
PPG = public or publicly guaranteed

Source: Birdsall, Claessens, and Diwan (2001).

unlikely to use the money well—they ended up using bilateral loans and grants to keep countries from defaulting on their official multilateral debt.

Thus the debt relief resulting from the HIPC Initiative may benefit donors as well as the HIPCs themselves. It may liberate donors that were previously locked into forced lending and permit them to restore country selectivity. This could lead to additional resources being provided to countries with more adequate policies and institutions, and thus increase the average efficiency of aid. And that in turn could help to restore the political will in donor countries to increase aid programs.

Summary

A large stock of accumulated debt can be an obstacle to growth and poverty reduction. Government officials have their freedom severely constrained by the need to keep aid flowing so as to be able to meet their debt-service obligations. They are forced to deal with dozens of creditors and donors proposing new projects involving new resource flows, and they are therefore likely to have difficulty planning and implementing the kind of sustained public investment programs in roads, schools, and other key sectors that would promote private investment, fuel growth, and address the needs of the poor.

Job-generating investment may be low because potential investors fear the future tax burden that high public debt implies in the absence of secure permanent net positive transfers from outside donors to government, or simply fear future economic and political uncertainty. Meanwhile, donors and creditors—to help governments avoid arrears on their high debt-service obligations, and to maintain the credibility and potential benefits of their favored programs—resort to a combination of debt rescheduling and fresh loans and grants that in fact represent few truly additional resources. The resulting process is not conducive to sustained development initiatives truly owned and managed by recipient governments.

Quite apart from the case for supplying these countries with more real resources, there is a case for thinking that transfer-neutral debt reduction could help get development moving again. And then there is the apparent political fact that it is easier for donors to muster political support to help countries in this way than through the more traditional channel of increasing the aid budget. No wonder we got an enhanced HIPC Initiative. The question to which we turn next is whether and how that initiative should be extended as a part of a program to revive the momentum of development.

5

Deepening and Extending Debt Reduction

We start from the premise that industrial countries should do more to help promote development in poor countries, because the evidence indicates that without more help poor countries will not achieve the Millennium Development Goals to which the world is ostensibly committed, even if all developing countries adopt good policies. It seems clear that the extra help needs to exceed by far any estimate of the savings of HIPCs in annual debt service under the enhanced HIPC Initiative, which we roughly suggested at the end of chapter 3 would be little more than $4 billion annually, even if all 42 eligible countries eventually reached completion points.

Debt campaigners have argued that the need to service debt has been a serious drain on the resources of low-income countries that has inevitably impeded their efforts to provide even minimal social services to their people and to develop their economies. Even though they have sometimes failed to acknowledge that the net resource flow to these economies has always remained positive, our analysis of the efficiency benefits of debt relief suggests that they were basically right in this argument. But some portion of those efficiency benefits, as well as the selectivity benefit we identify, has or will be reaped with the debt reduction that has by now happened, or that is due to happen, under the enhanced HIPC Initiative. Are further reductions warranted? Will they bring additionality, and if not, which other developing countries will pay for them?

This is the question that prevents us drawing the conclusion that all HIPC debt should be canceled. That might make sense if debt cancellation were the only politically feasible way of goading industrial countries into doing more. But given the likelihood that full debt cancellation would not lead to full additionality, there is a danger of diverting resources to countries where it would not necessarily be best used. Indeed, full debt cancellation altogether ignores the legitimate concern of the people in poor countries (and the debt campaigners) that future governments could waste or steal the resulting freed tax revenues and future creditors would more easily begin a new round of irresponsible lending. Complete debt cancellation for the HIPCs may not be the optimal way to advance development or increase the likelihood that the world's goal of at least halving poverty by 2015 will be achieved.

We do not claim to know the exact trade-off between the greater efficiency that deeper relief might bring and the perverse effects of any redistribution of total aid if additionality is less than complete. Instead, we ask what changes need to be made to the HIPC Initiative to make sure that debt is more predictably sustainable—so that it ceases to be a serious burden likely to impede the development process—in all the low-income countries. We suggest three avenues: deepening relief where necessary to ensure that a country's budget is not excessively burdened by debt-service payments; increasing the number of HIPC Initiative-eligible countries; and introducing a contingent mechanism to prevent debt sustainability from being undermined by circumstances beyond a country's own control. Our ideas for financing these proposals take into account our strong emphasis on maintaining intercountry equity.

Deeper Relief

The most profound of the criticisms leveled at the enhanced HIPC Initiative is that it has still got the key wrong, by focusing on the debt-export ratio as the primary measure of how much debt a country can afford to carry. If one is concerned about a country having to divert resources from basic social expenditures to servicing debt, then debt campaigners have argued that one should instead focus on what proportion of the resources available for government expenditure is preempted for debt service. For example, Oxfam (2001) has proposed that no low-income country should be expected to spend more than 10 percent of government revenue on debt service: debt should be canceled to the extent that it generates a higher burden than that. An even more profound departure from the current approach has been urged by Eurodad, in arguing for a country-by-country analysis of how much debt each country can afford to carry without preempting resources available for spending on a basic level of social service delivery.

The difficulty that we see with the Oxfam suggestion is the incentive that it gives a government to limit its search for tax revenue. Under the Oxfam formula, 10 percent of any extra tax revenue is immediately siphoned off for debt service. Perhaps 10 percent is not a high enough figure to generate a severe disincentive effect, but it is hard to be sure. And even if there is no disincentive effect, there is surely an equity effect: a country is rewarded for having failed to collect enough taxes to pay for a decent level of social expenditures. In any event, there seems to us to be a better formula. Instead of keying the debt-service ceiling to the level of tax revenue, why not key it directly to the level of GNP? This is one variable no government is going to suppress to minimize its debt-service bill, and it provides the best single estimate of the ability to afford social services.

Currently, the decision-point HIPCs collect about 20 percent of their GNP in tax revenue.[1] If one accepts the Oxfam figure for legitimate expenditure on debt service as a proportion of revenue, one would conclude that no country should be required to spend more than 10 percent of 20 percent of GNP—that is, 2 percent of GNP—on debt service to official debtors. If a country's debt is such as to generate official debt service of more than 2 percent of GNP, then the excess should be forgiven. Table 5.1 calculates the amount of additional debt reduction that would be needed in each of 11 HIPCs that have already passed the decision point to limit debt service on publicly guaranteed debt to 2 percent of GNP. (Debt service is already no more than 2 percent of GNP in the other 11 HIPCs that are past the decision point.)

The first two columns of table 5.1 show the projected debt stock and service at completion point. The next two columns show GNP and the present percentage of GNP spent on debt service. Then there is a column that shows the debt-service goal (2 percent of GNP), followed by one that calculates the corresponding debt-stock goal, assuming the same ratio of service to stock at the completion point. The final column shows the needed reduction in debt stock. According to the calculation, the cost would be $5.5 billion for the 11 of 24 decision-point HIPCs whose debt service currently exceeds 2 percent of GNP.

Because projections of debt stock and service at completion point are not available for HIPCs yet to reach the decision point, we make a rough estimate of the cost of debt reduction to the threshold of 2 percent of GNP for these countries. The first four columns of table 5.2 present the current debt stock, debt service, GNP, and exports for the 14 non-decision-point HIPCs.[2] The fifth column estimates a post-HIPC debt stock as 150

---

1. The average ratio of fiscal revenue (excluding grants) to GNP in 1999 for decision-point HIPCs was 19 percent, with a standard deviation of 7.5 (revenue data from World Bank 2001a; GNP from World Bank 2001b). The 20 percent figure is slightly less than in the United States and Japan, much less than in Europe, and somewhat above the average—but well below the peak—for developing countries.

2. This does not include the four HIPCs projected to reach sustainable levels of debt without receiving HIPC Initiative assistance. These four—Angola, Kenya, Vietnam, and Yemen—

Table 5.1 Additional reduction needed for post-decision point HIPCs that are above the 2 percent threshold
(billions of dollars)

	NPV of debt	Debt service	GDP	Ratio of debt service to GDP (percent)	Service goal	Stock goal	Stock reduction needed	IMF share[a]
Bolivia	1,649	260	8,660	3	173	1,098	551	33
Gambia	202	15	476	3.2	10	128	74	2
Guinea	1,254	78	2,239	3.5	45	720	534	21
Guyana	552	48	678	7.1	14	156	396	39
Honduras	2,912	204	6,649	2.5	133	1,898	1,014	48
Malawi	767	45	1,565	2.9	31	533	234	8
Mali	994	64	2,813	2.3	56	874	120	8
Mauritania	612	108	2,400	4.5	48	272	340	16
Nicaragua	1,320	116	2,231	5.2	45	508	812	21
Senegal	2,149	174	5,553	3.1	111	1,372	777	62
Zambia	2,231	151	4,059	3.7	81	1,199	1,032	213
Total							**5,883**	**471**

NPV = net present value

a. Hypothetical cost to the IMF based on current share of outstanding debt.

Note: Figures for Bolivia and Malawi include additional pledged bilateral assistance.

Source: HIPC decision-point documents. All figures are post-HIPC assistance.

Table 5.2 Cost to bring all non-decision point HIPCs below the 2 percent debt-to-GNP threshold
(millions of dollars)

Country	NPV of debt[a]	Debt service	GNP	Exports	Post-HIPC debt stock	Ratio of debt service to GNP	Reduction needed	IMF share[b]
Burundi	639	27	705	79	119	0.7	n.a.	
Central African Republic	528	17	1,035	157	236	0.7	n.a.	
Comoros	120	7	193	45	67	2.0	1	
Congo, Democratic Republic of	8,022	3	n.a.	1,561	2,342	0.0	n.a.	
Congo, Republic of	3,748	5	1,662	1,700	2,550	0.2	n.a.	
Côte d'Ivoire	9,459	1,003	10,425	5,272	5,625	5.7	3,659	220
Ghana	4,304	468	7,634	2,309	2,204	3.1	800	44
Lao PDR	1,382	37	1,393	469	704	1.4	n.a.	
Liberia	1,318	3	n.a.	n.a.	n.a.	n.a.	n.a.	
Myanmar	3,998	88	n.a.	1,655	2,483	n.a.	n.a.	
Sierra Leone	806	21	652	77	115	0.5	n.a.	
Somalia	1,796	1	n.a.	n.a.	n.a.	n.a.	n.a.	
Sudan	8,973	57	8,819	716	1,074	0.1	n.a.	
Togo	1,004	36	1,380	539	809	2.1	39	3
Total							**4,498**	**247**

n.a. = not applicable

NPV = net present value

a. The NPV of publicly guaranteed debt is calculated by discounting the nominal public or publicly guaranteed debt figures by the ratio of nominal to net present value of total outstanding debt presented in GDF, table A1.4.

b. Hypothetical cost to the IMF based on the current share of outstanding debt.

Note: The post-HIPC debt stock (fifth column) assumes a 150 percent debt-export ratio and the hypothetical post-HIPC ratio of debt service to GNP (sixth column) assumes a constant ratio of debt stock to debt service.

Source: World Bank, *Global Development Finance* CD-ROM, 2001 (GDF).

percent of exports, and the sixth calculates the ratio of debt service to GNP that such a stock would yield, again holding the ratio of service to stock constant. All but three of the countries—Côte d'Ivoire, Ghana, and Togo—would already fall below the threshold of 2 percent of GNP. The cost of additional debt reduction for these three countries is estimated at $4.5 billion. Our total estimate to reach the 2 percent threshold for the HIPCs is thus $10 billion.[3]

Consider next the alternative Eurodad proposal for limiting debt service to what it calculates each country can afford to pay. Table 5.3 shows the cost of this proposal. Total resources consist of tax revenue plus grants, whereas minimum essential spending consists of social expenditures that vary between $40 and $95 per head, plus domestic debt service. The difference between the two is the remaining resources reckoned to be available for such inessential expenditures as servicing foreign debt. Affordable foreign debt service is then one-third of those remaining resources. This is compared with the actual level of debt service paid abroad.

In the majority of cases, actual debt service exceeds the affordable level, leading Eurodad to advocate sufficient debt-service relief to reduce actual service to the affordable level. But in 5 of the 21 cases, affordable debt service exceeds actual service so that there is no need for further relief, whereas in 7 cases its calculation of affordable service is zero and additional grants (shown by the superscript a) would be needed to allow the countries to provide a minimum level of social services. The additional needs as calculated by Eurodad are $638 million in debt-service relief and $795 million in additional new grants, a total of slightly more than $1.4 billion. The final column then shows the reduction in the net present value of the debt stock that would be required to generate the required level of debt-service relief, assuming that the debt-stock reduction is proportional to the debt-service reduction. This sums to $11.8 billion.

This cost is slightly more than that of our proposal to reduce debt stock to a level that will generate debt service of no more than 2 percent of GNP, which would, we estimated, cost about $10 billion in additional debt relief. But cost is not the issue. The really interesting feature of table 5.3 is that it shows that Eurodad calculates that achievement of their target would actually require a greater increase in grants than reduction

---

together represent 44 percent of the total outstanding debt of the HIPCs, but most of this debt, especially in the cases of Angola and Vietnam, is held by bilateral creditors and will be reduced with traditional Paris Club mechanisms according to Naples terms.

3. This estimate does not take into account additional bilateral debt reduction (in some cases a 100 percent write-off) that has been pledged by some European governments because data on these pledges are not yet available. This additional bilateral reduction has been estimated at $8 billion (personal communication with the World Bank HIPC unit). Although bilateral reductions of this kind would ease pressure on the multilaterals to provide additional debt relief, they still represent an additional "cost" to the donor community.

Table 5.3 Cost of Eurodad proposal for limiting debt service (millions of dollars)

Country	Total resources	Essential spending	Remaining resources	Affordable debt service	Actual debt service	Additional resources needed		NPV of debt stock	Needed debt reduction
						Debt service reduction	Grant increase		
Benin	543	419	124	37	46	8	0	685	123
Bolivia	2,300	1,224	1,076	323	185	0	0	1,672	0
Burkina Faso	614	644	0	0	30	30	30[a]	233	233
Cameroon	1,961	1,427	534	160	226	66	0	5,341	1,549
Gambia	96	191	0	0	16	16	95[a]	191	499
Guinea	521	438	83	25	78	53	0	1,870	130
Guinea-Bissau	90	122	0	0	6	6	31[a]	293	1,870
Guyana	348	280	68	20	48	27	0	282	161
Honduras	1,353	496	858	257	134	0	0	2,740	0
Madagascar	854	722	132	40	64	25	0	2,129	809
Malawi	558	750	0	0	59	59	193[a]	839	839
Mali	661	534	127	38	64	26	0	906	376
Mauritania	436	218	217	65	80	15	0	945	170
Mozambique	1,145	930	215	65	48	0	0	761	0
Nicaragua	938	546	392	118	108	0	0	2,274	0
Niger	325	578	0	0	28	28	253[a]	568	568
Rwanda	374	352	22	7	16	9	0	244	142
Senegal	1,168	620	548	164	159	0	0	2,007	0
Tanzania	1,626	1,816	0	0	142	142	190[a]	2,587	2,587
Uganda	1,251	1,253	0	0	48	48	3[a]	745	745
Zambia	895	738	157	47	136	89	0	1,575	1,024
Total						647	795		11,825

NPV = net present value

a. Needed increase in grants to supplement elimination of debt service.

Source: Eurodad (2001a).

in debt service. In other words, even a dedicated group of debt campaigners has been driven to the conclusion that further debt relief is inherently unable to deliver all that is needed.

One curiosity of table 5.3: It shows that the country that would get the largest increase in grant aid is Niger, which is a rather small country of about 10 million people but nevertheless is awarded almost a quarter billion dollars of extra grant aid. This is not because Eurodad projects Niger's social expenditure needs to be particularly high; the figure is actually slightly below Eurodad's average for per capita expenditure needs.[4] Rather, Niger is an outlier because it raises less tax revenue as a percentage of GDP (only 10.2 percent) than any other HIPC. Does one really want to reward countries for failing to get their citizens to pay a reasonable level of taxes?[5]

This indicates the basic problem with the Eurodad suggestion: the likelihood that it would divert funding away from other low-income countries toward the HIPCs irrespective of the relative quality of countries' tax effort and spending allocations. This is much more than a hypothetical danger. The increasing dependence on aid of the heavily indebted poor countries, primarily in Africa, has played a role in reducing aid to India (from 1.5 percent of its GNP a decade ago to as little as 0.1 percent currently), despite the fact that India's tax and spending programs are relatively reasonable and its record in reducing poverty much better than that of most of the HIPCs. We conclude that our proposal to use 2 percent of GNP for debt service as a benchmark is both more straightforward and transparent, and more supportive of countries' own efforts.

Making More Countries Eligible

We have emphasized our conviction that most debt campaigners have overlooked the distributional implications of their proposals for debt cancellation. We have identified the channels through which the reduction of some countries' debt could come at the cost of other low-income countries: by diverting bilateral aid from non-HIPCs to HIPCs, by inducing a rise in the interest charges of the multilateral development banks, and by reducing new IDA lending. We have argued that maintaining the trust fund to finance HIPC debt reduction, rather than raiding World Bank reserves, is an important way to limit redistribution. Nevertheless, it is

---

4. Another problem with the Eurodad proposal is the likely difficulty in reaching international agreement on a formula that awarded different per capita expenditure requirements to different countries.

5. Van de Walle (2001) argues that dependence on donors has allowed some African governments to avoid the accountability to their citizens that a tax system creates.

Table 5.4 Debt indicators for potential HIPCs, 1999 (percent)

Country	Ratio of NPV of debt-to-exports	Ratio of NPV of debt-to-GNP	Ratio of debt service to exports	Ratio of debt service to government revenue	Ratio of debt service to GNP
Armenia	135	42	11	n.a.	2.9
Azerbaijan	49	18	6	11	2.3
Bangladesh	134	23	10	n.a.	1.6
Cambodia	157	59	3	n.a.	1.0
Georgia[a]	136	45	11	33	3.7
Haiti	113	15	10	n.a.	1.3
Indonesia	140	62	16	37	7.2
Kyrgyzstan	177	81	5	17	2.2
Moldova	120	70	24	n.a.	14.3
Nigeria	142	70	5	n.a.	2.7
Pakistan	219	37	19	19	3.2
Sri Lanka[a]	104	45	7	19	3.2
Tajikistan	36	29	4	n.a.	1.6
Turkmenistan[a]	116	54	30	n.a.	14.0
Uzbekistan	114	10	16	n.a.	n.a.
Zimbabwe	125	61	22	n.a.	10.5

n.a. = not available

NPV = net present value

a. Lower-middle-income countries.

Note: Public and publicly guaranteed debt only.

Source: World Bank, Global Development Finance (2001).

not possible to be certain that no redistribution will occur, especially through the redirection of bilateral aid.

A way of limiting inadvertent redistribution is to include more countries in the HIPC Initiative. Compare a situation in which all outstanding HIPC debt is canceled with another in which the same value of debt is canceled but by reducing the debt service of all low-income countries to x percent of GNP. In the former case, the benefit of debt relief is concentrated on the present HIPCs; in the latter case, it would be more widely distributed, and therefore less likely to penalize the countries that would be excluded under the former approach.

The danger of giving complete debt relief to a limited group of countries is that the countries that built up the deepest debt problems in the past are likely to include the countries that were most prone to waste external resources. We therefore believe that there is a strong case for making virtually all low-income countries eligible for inclusion in the HIPC Initiative.

Tables 5.4 and 5.5 give critical debt statistics for two other groups of countries. Table 5.4 contains the statistics for 16 countries that we have

Table 5.5 Debt statistics for other low-income countries, 1999
               (percent)

Country	Ratio of NPV of debt-to-exports	Ratio of NPV of debt-to-GNP	Ratio of debt service to exports	Ratio of debt service to government revenue	Ratio of debt service to GNP
Afghanistan	n.a.	n.a.	n.a.	n.a.	n.a.
Eritrea	71	19	2	n.a.	1.0
India	91	13	13	16	1.9
Lesotho	91	45	9	n.a.	4.6
Mongolia	91	57	5	14	2.9
Nepal	120	32	8	21	2.0

n.a. = not available

NPV = net present value

Source: World Bank, *Global Development Finance* (2001).

seen mentioned as candidates for HIPC status, either by debt campaigners or (in the case of economies in transition) in a recent British proposal. Table 5.5 contains similar statistics for the 6 other low-income countries with populations of more than 1.5 million that belong to the IMF and World Bank.

Three of the countries in table 5.4 (Georgia, Sri Lanka, and Turkmenistan) are lower-middle-income countries rather than low-income (i.e., their GNP per capita, converted at the market exchange rate, exceeded $755 in 2000). It is true that two of the existing HIPCs, namely Bolivia and Guyana, are also lower-middle-income countries. Tables 2.3 and 2.4 above shows that both of these were indeed very heavily indebted countries. Of the three lower-middle-income countries in table 5.4, none is comparably overindebted: although the debt-GNP ratios of both Georgia and Sri Lanka are more than 40 percent, they are only modestly more. It is true that seven HIPCs have lower debt-GNP ratios, but these are all much poorer countries. We therefore propose not considering Georgia, Sri Lanka, or Turkmenistan as candidates for an extended HIPC program.

Only three of the remaining 22 countries listed in tables 5.4 and 5.5 have a debt-export ratio above the HIPC threshold of 150 percent: Cambodia, Kyrgyzstan, and Pakistan. This group's indebtedness looks more severe according to the criterion of debt stock to GNP, whereby 12 of the 22 exceed the 40 percent norm. Ratios of debt service to exports exceed the 15 percent norm in 6 cases. Statistics for debt service to government revenue exist for only 9 of the 22 countries, and Indonesia's is more than 30 percent. The ratio of debt service to GNP looks quite high relative to the existing HIPCs, especially relative to the post-debt-relief levels shown in the final column of table 2.4. All but six are at or above the 2 percent maximum for the ratio of debt service to GNP that we suggested in the previous section, while 7 countries exceed the 4.1 percent pre-debt-relief average for the existing HIPCs.

Although few of these countries suffer an external debt problem as severe as those of the existing HIPCs before they received relief, we believe that they should be brought on board if debt relief for existing HIPCs is to be deepened as proposed above. To do otherwise would be to penalize these countries for having conducted their affairs prudently in the past,[6] and probably to redirect some aid away from countries where it would be more effective in reducing poverty. That would be both unjust and quite probably—to the extent that countries with bad policies in the past continue to have bad policies in the future—inefficient.

How much would it cost to reduce the public or publicly guaranteed (PPG) debt of these 22 countries to a level that would cut their debt-export ratio to 150 percent and their external PPG debt service to 2 percent of GNP (the levels that we selected as desirable targets in the case of the existing HIPCs)? Table 5.6 shows our estimates of the cost of extending the HIPC Initiative to all other low-income countries. We lack data for Afghanistan and Uzbekistan. Six of the remaining 17 already fall below both thresholds and would therefore not be entitled to any debt reduction. The cost for the remaining 11 is estimated in two steps. First is the reduction in bilateral debt that these countries would receive under Paris Club Naples terms treatment. Receiving Naples terms from the Paris Club is a prerequisite for consideration under the current HIPC Initiative. This cost would be borne by bilateral creditors according to their share of debt owed by these countries. Second is the cost under HIPC terms (burden sharing across all creditors) of a post-Naples reduction to the threshold of a 2 percent ratio of debt service to GNP or the threshold of a 150 percent ratio of debt to exports.

The extension of Paris Club Naples terms would cost bilateral creditors about $39 billion (column E of the table). Naples treatment would bring four countries—Azerbaijan, Kyrgyzstan, Nepal, and Nigeria—under the 2 percent threshold. Additional debt relief for the remaining seven countries would cost another $41.5 billion (column K). Columns L-O estimate the cost to the different creditors that this $41 billion ticket would entail. Private debt with a public guarantee makes up about $11.5 billion, debt owed to bilateral creditors $8 billion, and debt owed to multilateral creditors $22 billion. This means that the overall cost to official creditors of bringing these non-HIPCs under the 2 percent threshold is about $69 billion ($47 billion bilateral and $22 billion multilateral).

---

6. In some cases, this record of past prudence has been violated more recently, but it is still true that it was earlier prudence that qualified a country like Pakistan to be a blend country, which then disqualified it as a HIPC candidate under the decision that HIPCs be limited to countries with IDA-only status.

Table 5.6 Cost to bring all low-income countries below the 2 percent threshold for debt service to GNP and 150 percent threshold for debt to exports (in millions)

	(A)	(B)	(C)	(D) Share of outstanding PPG debt (percent)			(E)	(F)	(G) Share of outstanding PPG debt (percent)			(H)	(I)	(K)	(L)	(M)	(N)	(O)	(P)
Country	GNP	NPV of debt	Debt service	Bilat-eral	Multi-lateral	Pri-vate	Hypo-thetical Naples-terms treatment	Post-Naples-terms debt stock	Bilat-eral	Multi-lateral	Pri-vate	Post-Naples debt service	Ratio of debt service to GNP	Stock reduction needed	Bilat-eral cost	Cost via multi-lateral trust funds	IMF share	Cost to private sector	Total bilat-eral cost (E+L)
Armenia	1,919	627	56	26	74	0	106	521	10	90	0	47	2.4	91	10	82	25	0	116
Azerbaijan	3,449	646	78	18	77	5	79	567	7	87	6	69	2.0	n.a.	n.a.	n.a.	n.a.	n.a.	n.a.
Indonesia	132,467	82,250	9,558	42	36	21	22,994	59,256	20	50	30	6,886	5.2	36,458	7,288	18,323	6,263	10,847	30,282
Kyrgyzstan	1,175	953	26	33	65	2	208	745	14	83	3	20	1.7	n.a.	n.a.	n.a.	n.a.	n.a.	n.a.
Lesotho	1,110	494	51	18	74	8	58	436	7	84	9	45	4.1	221	15	185	6	21	73
Moldova	1,196	843	171	23	63	14	126	717	9	74	17	145	12.2	599	54	446	137	99	180
Mongolia	862	492	25	41	56	2	134	358	19	77	3	18	2.1	19	4	15	2	1	138
Nepal	5,155	1,627	105	12	87	1	128	1,499	4	95	1	97	1.9	n.a.	n.a.	n.a.	n.a.	n.a.	n.a.
Nigeria	31,432	21,811	835	58	17	26	8,282	13,529	32	27	41	518	1.6	2,328	437	1,665	179	226	6,288
Pakistan	58,817	21,912	1,877	40	52	7	5,851	16,061	19	72	10	1,376	2.3	1,866	280	1,341	249	244	1,002
Zimbabwe	5,234	3,195	551	34	56	10	722	2,473	15	72	13	427	8.1	n.a.	n.a.	n.a.	n.a.	n.a.	n.a.
Total							38,688							41,582	8,088	22,057	6,861	11,438	46,776

n.a. = not applicable

NPV = net present value

PPG = public or publicly guaranteed

Note: In all cases, the post-Naples debt stock (column F) brings the debt-export ratio below 150 percent, therefore making the ratio of debt service to GNP the binding constraint. Column E calculates a hypothetical 67 percent Naples terms reduction on bilateral debt; column H is calculated assuming a constant ratio of debt service to stock. Column K shows the stock reduction needed after Naples terms to get countries below the 2 percent threshold in column I. Columns L–O break down this reduction by creditor.

Source: World Bank, Global Development Finance CD-ROM, 2001. Debt-stock and service data refer to public and publicly guaranteed debt only, and all figures are presented in NPV terms. 'Stock reduction needed' is calculated assuming a constant stock-service ratio, and the costs to official creditors are calculated assuming a constant burden-sharing arrangement based on the current composition of outstanding debt.

This scenario envisages the possibility of seven small countries qualifying for debt reduction of less than $1 billion each. The amount would be larger for Zimbabwe ($2.6 billion), although it seems in tragically little likelihood of qualifying in the near future. Nigeria would be entitled to $8.3 billion under Naples terms, which we assume it would take as soon as it could, because it has been requesting debt relief ever since the military despot that used to rule it was replaced. Pakistan would have been entitled to $8.2 billion, before its December 2001 Paris Club agreement, which already reduced the NPV of its debt stock by about $3 billion. Pakistan would also be obliged to seek further relief of $249 million from its private creditors if the principle of comparable sacrifice of the official and private sectors were strictly maintained, which might jeopardize its relations with its private creditors who have already agreed to one restructuring. This was presented as an argument against seeking debt relief by a committee that examined Pakistan's debt problems last year (Debt Reduction and Management Committee 2001).

The really big-ticket sum, however—nearly $60 billion—relates to Indonesia ($11 billion of which would be borne by the private sector). Indonesia accounts for no less than 75 percent of the total cost to official creditors of providing debt relief to all 19 countries—more than twice the cost of the entire enhanced HIPC Initiative. Given how indebted Indonesia is, one cannot assume that it would not apply for debt relief.

The case of Indonesia sharply points up the dilemma of debt relief. Its inclusion would result in a major escalation in the cost of our proposals, from $30 billion plus ($10 billion for deepening, $20 billion for expanding to other low-income non-HIPCs, plus the cost of the contingency facility) without participation by Indonesia, to a total of about $79 billion plus. Until its implosion following the Thai crisis in 1997, Indonesia was a fairly heavily indebted lower-middle-income country but appeared to be making good use of the resources it borrowed and to be capable of carrying its debt load.

But contagion hit Indonesia with a vengeance, and capital flight led to severe currency depreciation after the rupiah was allowed to float, magnifying foreign-currency-denominated debts to a point where large swaths of the economy became insolvent. The consequences include a decline in income to levels that have carried the country back into the ranks of low-income countries and a major increase in the burden imposed by external debt. Surely this is a country that desperately needs the sort of debt relief that is provided by the HIPC Initiative, and its past record even under a corrupt government suggests it has the institutional capacity to make good use of it. We find the case for making Indonesia eligible to be compelling, especially given its turn to democracy.

A Contingency Facility

One of the grounds on which the analysis underlying the HIPC Initiative has been justifiably criticized by the debt campaigners is that it uses overoptimistic assumptions to support the conclusion that the scaled-down debt of the HIPCs is now sustainable. Our own analysis of this issue in chapter 3 concluded that the assumptions, though not ludicrous, are certainly on the optimistic side. This is especially serious because low-income countries tend to be particularly susceptible to exogenous shocks to export prices and to the climate, and in some cases to import prices as well. The IMF has accepted this in principle, and it is currently estimated that the 21 countries between decision and completion points may be entitled to another $500 million topping up at the completion point. But that still leaves them vulnerable to such shocks occurring after the completion point.

We propose that this should be corrected by creating an ability to grant additional relief if shocks that are clearly exogenous to the country result in a new erosion of debt sustainability.[7] Technically, this would require a mechanism for identifying when a country had suffered an exogenous shock and for quantifying its balance of payments effects, as well as a fund that would finance the additional relief.

The way in which exogenous shocks should be identified is by explicitly specifying the expectations about the key exogenous variables that affect poor countries' balances of payments at the time HIPC relief is agreed to. For most countries, these will be the terms of trade (i.e., the price of exports relative to that of imports), market growth, and the climate. Expectations about the first are already quantified in the debt-sustainability analyses that have been undertaken by the World Bank-IMF HIPC unit. Expected market growth is implicitly (in most cases) the projected growth rate of export volume. Nor is it difficult to identify climatic events that seriously affect balance of payments outcomes: frosts that kill coffee crops or hurricanes that ravage a country's infrastructure are not state secrets. Quantifying the effects of a departure from expectations would be an essentially technical exercise, although there will always be scope for debate at the margin (nor is there any way to dictate ex ante the complete insulation of the process from political pressures).

This kind of insurance against exogenous shocks would need to cover a substantial period into the future, at least a decade,[8] if it were to serve the role of reassuring investors that the public sector's debt burden is

---

7. Such contingent facilities are not completely new to the international system. For many years, the IMF has operated a Contingency Financing Facility that lends (though it does not grant) money to IMF member countries experiencing a shortfall in export proceeds due to circumstances outside their control. Similarly, the Mexican bonds issued under the Brady Plan included contingent payments to their holders that allowed them to benefit if the price of Mexican oil exports exceeded a benchmark level.

8. But probably it ought not to cover much more than a decade, so as not to create moral hazard (by destroying a country's incentive to diversify its economy to reduce its vulnerability to exogenous shocks).

sustainable. It is impossible to cost such a facility ex ante, because the outlay will depend upon the particular size and sequence of shocks to which the countries are subjected. Nevertheless, the $500 million expected cost of topping up for the 20 decision-point HIPCs at completion point gives some idea of what the actual cost would be, admittedly during a world recession that has weakened commodity prices. Thus $5 billion would be a pessimistic estimate of the cost for these 20 countries over 10 years. Considering that 10 of the remaining 12 HIPC-eligible countries yet to reach the decision point are highly dependent on commodity exports, a cost of $5 billion for the entire set of HIPCs over 10 years may be optimistic.[9]

Another way to get a sense of the hypothetical cost of such a contingency facility is to suppose that the value of each HIPC's exports for the next decade rose only at the same rate as in the 1990s (or remained flat, for countries whose exports declined in the past). Suppose also that this occurred because of much less favorable developments in the terms of trade than were assumed in the World Bank-IMF study, which would qualify as an exogenous development. Our calculation as to how much this would cost is shown in table 5.7, where it can be seen that the cost would be about $5.2 billion for the 24 post-decision-point countries. Of course, it is not likely that all countries would end up mirroring the experience of the 1990s—perhaps equally unlikely as their achieving 8.2 percent annual export growth—but the estimate again suggests that $5 billion may be an optimistic figure for the cost of such a procedure for all HIPCs.

Because the IMF already has a great deal of experience in operating a contingency facility that requires similar expertise, it would be natural to locate such a facility there. Every year, the IMF would calculate whether each HIPC's debt-export ratio exceeded 150 percent. If it did, then it would examine whether the excess (or how much of the excess) could be attributed to shocks to the terms of trade, low market growth, bad weather, or other factors that could reasonably be considered exogenous, as compared with the baseline that had been previously established. These country analyses would be made available to the public. If a country's debts had increased in relation to its exports because of circumstances beyond its control, then the IMF would provide the resources to reduce the debt to 150 percent of exports, perhaps by paying IDA or other multilaterals to write off the requisite amount of IDA debt. We discuss subsequently where this money should come from.

Financing More Debt Relief

The program that we have proposed above would not be cheap. Figure 5.1 compares the cost to official creditors of our proposals as compared

---

9. The extra countries that we are suggesting adding are mostly much less vulnerable to commodity shocks.

Table 5.7 Hypothetical cost of contingency procedure (in millions)

	HIPC export projections		Export growth (1990-99 average)	Revised export projections (2010, based on 1990s growth)	2010 debt stock (HIPC projection)	Debt-to-export ratio (revised)	Stock goal (at 150 percent)	Reduction
	2001	2010						
Benin	392	791	2.5	489	795	1.63	734	62
Bolivia	1,442	3,108	3.6	2,054	3,333	1.62	3,081	252
Burkina Faso	305	751	−2.6	305	1,024	3.36	458	567
Cameroon	2,586	4,248	0.0	2,586	4,248	1.64	3,879	369
Chad	242	1,978	0.6	255	934	3.66	383	552
Ethiopia	952	1,815	2.6	1,199	2,439	2.03	1,799	641
Gambia	128	233	2.7	163	301	1.85	245	57
Guinea	860	1,647	−1.0	860	1,565	1.82	1,290	275
Guinea-Bissau	71	181	7.5	136	248	1.82	204	44
Guyana	718	1,037	5.0	1,114	736	0.66	n.a.	n.a.
Honduras[a]	2,673	5,456	8.5	4,361	3,323	0.76	n.a.	n.a.
Madagascar	1,046	1,811	6.5	1,731	1,929	1.11	n.a.	n.a.
Malawi	480	763	2.1	579	1,148	1.98	869	280
Mali	662	1,190	2.3	812	1,520	1.87	1,218	302
Mauritania[b]	433	528	−2.5	433	656	1.52	650	7
Mozambique	805	3,451	6.8	1,455	1,611	1.11	n.a.	n.a.
Nicaragua[a]	932	1,570	10.0	1,651	1,712	1.04	n.a.	n.a.
Niger	279	484	−4.5	279	768	2.75	419	350
Rwanda	126	367	−3.0	126	541	4.29	189	352
São Tomé and Principe	18	42	5.0	28	59	2.11	42	17
Senegal	1,692	2,765	−1.0	1,692	2,364	1.40	n.a.	n.a.
Tanzania[a]	1,194	2,274	7.9	1,884	3,525	1.87	2,826	699
Uganda	801	1,953	11.5	2,134	1,320	0.62	n.a.	n.a.
Zambia	1,038	2,207	−3.0	1,036	2,575	2.49	1,554	1,021
Total[c]								5,292

n.a. = not applicable

a. Stock in 2007.

b. Stock in 2006.

c. Chad is excluded from the total because of the likely increases in exports due to exploitation of oil reserves.

Source: World Bank, *Global Development Finance* CD-ROM (2001), and HIPC Debt Sustainability Analysis (DSA) documents.

Figure 5.1   Cost estimates to public sector

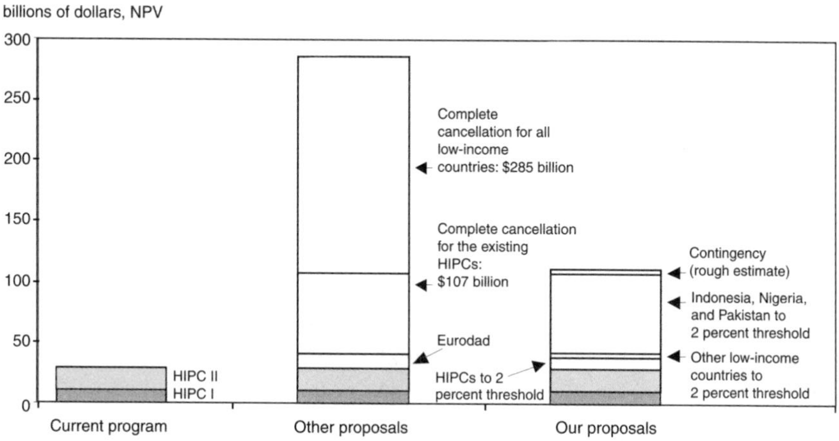

billions of dollars, NPV

NPV = net present value

Note: HIPC I is the HIPC Initiative; HIPC II is the enhanced initiative.

Source: Authors' calculations.

with certain other proposals. The first bar shows the cost of the HIPC Initiative (HIPC I) and the enhanced initiative (HIPC II). The second bar adds to them the cost of the two main proposals tabled by the debt campaigners: the Eurodad proposal and the proposal to cancel all the debt of the existing HIPCs. It also shows the cost of an even more ambitious proposal, to cancel all the debt of all the low-income countries.

The figure's third bar again starts by presenting the cost of HIPC I and HIPC II, and then adds the cost to official creditors of our three proposals: to bring all the existing HIPCs down to a maximum ratio of debt service to GNP of 2 percent ($10 billion); to expand HIPC Initiative eligibility to all other low-income countries (shown separately for the smaller debtors—$4 billion—and then for Indonesia, Nigeria, and Pakistan—$64 billion); and to create a contingency facility ($5 billion). The total cost of this proposal would be comparable to the most ambitious proposals of the debt campaigners, but the distribution of the benefits would be very different, with the extra benefits accruing to other debt-burdened low-income countries rather than existing HIPCs. We now consider various ways in which additional debt relief could be financed, and then summarize our specific proposal.

IMF Gold Mobilization

As was described above, the IMF has already used an off-market gold transaction to mobilize a sum of $3.9 billion, the interest from which helped finance the IMF's share of HIPC relief. That transaction involved a mere 14 percent of the IMF's gold holding, which in total amounts to some 10 percent of the world's monetary gold. Because gold has long since ceased to serve any serious monetary function, IMF members could at any time agree to use additional IMF-held gold in the same way. It is true that this would amount to reducing the IMF's reserves, but, unlike the multilateral development banks, the IMF does not need a reserve to reassure lenders and thus permit it to borrow cheaply. The only function of the IMF gold stock is to reassure central bankers that their funds are safe with the IMF. We believe that the needs of the HIPCs and other poor countries are many times more compelling than safeguarding against the contingency of central bank irrationality.

An economist might argue that it would be preferable to mobilize this gold by a straightforward sale rather than by replicating the off-market transaction used in 1999, because that would release real resources to finance the debt cancellation. Such a sale might raise around $21 billion, if all the gold were sold and the sale depressed the gold price from its present level by 10 percent. This operation would require support by 85 percent of the IMF board, which means that US support would be essential for such an operation to be approved.

But it may prove politically easier to mobilize gold by further off-market transactions, which would not offend gold producers by threatening to reduce the gold price. This would also have the advantage of releasing somewhat more money (about $23 billion at the current price).

Some would argue that—despite the possible resistance in the US Congress to mobilizing IMF gold (or the complication that Congress would insist on other reforms at the IMF in exchange for its approval)—using gold is all too easy and cheap an escape for the donors. We do not think this logic warrants rejecting the use of gold altogether. Debt relief (and new transfers) have large potential benefits for reducing poverty, even if they do not appear to "cost" the traditional donors anything. In any event, the donor community could tie its own hands by linking gold mobilization for debt reduction to rising ODA disbursements, to avoid the gold becoming an easy out or, worse, a substitute for new donor commitments.[10]

---

10. Soros (2001) has urged that the IMF revive periodic issues of its fiat reserve asset, the Special Drawing Right (SDR), and use the proceeds to finance additional aid to developing countries. The SDR now carries a commercial interest rate (equal to the average short-term interest rate in the currencies that compose the SDR basket); he suggests that SDRs be issued to all IMF members in accordance with their quotas as provided in the IMF's Articles of Agreement, and then that the industrial countries donate their share for distribution to developing countries. They would presumably retain responsibility for paying the interest service, or would appropriate resources in their budgets at the moment of exchanging the SDRs for dollars or other currencies. We do not include this proposal because it is equivalent to a straightforward increase in donor aid budgets, though we note that it would have the advantage of providing a built-in answer to the question as to how the burden of additional relief would be spread among the industrial countries: They would bear the burden in proportion to their IMF quotas.

Increased Donor ODA

Even allowing for the possibility that Pakistan and perhaps Indonesia would not avail themselves of any debt relief offered to them, it is clear that the cost of the more ambitious of these proposals is large. In particular, extension of debt relief to Indonesia on terms similar to those that we have argued would be appropriate for the existing HIPCs would be possible only if the donors were prepared to increase ODA substantially. In principle, there is plenty of scope for this: if all the donors achieved the UN aid target of 0.7 percent of GNP, the annual flow of aid would increase from about $56 billion now to $160 billion. Although the debt relief to which Indonesia would be entitled is massive relative to the scale of the existing HIPC Initiative, it would take less than a year's increment to the aid flow to provide that level of relief to Indonesia.

An increase in ODA would occur semiautomatically if the donors maintained their ODA disbursements at a constant level while high-income members of the Paris Club granted Cologne terms (or better) on the bilateral debt of the additional countries admitted to an expanded HIPC program. This is what we recommend. The reduction of bilateral debt would then increase ODA during the following years, as long as new disbursements were unaffected. Reduction of the multilateral debt would need to be financed by increased donor contributions to the trust fund, which would need to come from an increase in new ODA disbursements, if debt relief for some were not to be at the expense of other developing countries. (If one believes that HIPC Initiative-inspired reforms like the introduction of Poverty Reduction Strategy Papers have now created the conditions for larger aid flows to be effective, it is particularly important to ensure that other poor countries with decent institutions and policies are not inadvertently squeezed out by expanded debt relief.)

Higher Multilateral Bank Charges

Although an inadvertent passing of the burden of HIPC relief to other low-income countries as a result of drawing down the World Bank's reserves should be strongly resisted, that is not to deny the case for deliberately increasing the interest rate charged to the World Bank's middle-income borrowers. Such a step was urged by a commission sponsored by the Carnegie Endowment for International Peace (2001).[11] The commission's report on the future of the multilateral development banks argued that such higher interest rates were a way to encourage countries to self-

---

11. One of the authors of this study directed the work of the commission, and both participated as members. The commission was cochaired by Angel Gurria of Mexico and Paul Volcker of the United States.

graduate. They would also raise the profits of these banks, which would enable them to funnel increased support to the HIPC program (the World Bank already provides $200 million a year). Given that about $92 billion of the IBRD's outstanding loan portfolio of $118 billion is lent to middle-income countries, this might yield the World Bank about $460 million a year if the interest rate were raised by 0.5 percent. If the higher interest rate were charged only to upper-middle-income countries (those with a per capita income above $2,995 a year), the annual yield would be $235 million. If the same pricing approach were adopted by the regional development banks as well, we estimate that the annual yield would be about $200 million.[12]

No country could be expected to welcome the prospect of paying higher interest charges for its loans. If the upper-middle-income countries were asked to bear the greater part of the burden of financing further debt relief for poor countries without the rich countries increasing their ODA, they would surely have a legitimate grudge. But if this action were to be taken in concert with higher ODA levels by the industrial countries (perhaps excluding the five that already reach the 0.7 percent target), one could hope that the upper-middle-income countries would accept it gracefully as their part of an international compact.[13]

Summary

First, by mobilizing its gold (through the off-market transaction already used once), the IMF is in a position to finance its own role in an expanded debt relief effort. That role would involve some further write-down in PRGF loans, mainly to help some of the existing HIPCs achieve the maximum ratio of 2 percent of GDP being devoted to debt service (about $1 billion). In addition, seven of the countries on our list of potential new HIPCs had PRGF loans to reduce as of October 2001, totaling about $900 million. IMF loans to Indonesia and Pakistan are much larger, and writing them down as part of an expanded HIPC Initiative could cost the IMF $7 billion.

We have also suggested that the IMF should be responsible for operating the contingency facility that would provide assurance that HIPCs will not go back above a 150 percent debt-export ratio as a result of circumstances beyond their control for the next 10 years. It is in principle impossible to forecast the cost of such a facility, but experience with the existing HIPCs suggests that it might be of the order of $5 billion. That again appears well within the capacity of the IMF to fund via gold. The IMF members' gold could in this way play an important role in relieving the burden imposed

---

12. The loan portfolio of middle-income countries and upper-middle-income countries in the regional banks is currently $90 billion and $38 billion respectively.

13. The Carnegie-sponsored commission also noted that the middle-income countries might then also expect a greater role in collective decisions about use of the additional net income.

by debt on the poorest countries (while leaving open the possibility that the IMF might even end up with as much as $12 billion of its $21 billion gold stock intact, if things turn out as well as its own forecasts suggest).

But the largest contribution must come from securing a major increase in the flow of ODA from donors. Some bilateral donors have already pledged a complete debt write-off to HIPCs in addition to participating in the enhanced HIPC Initiative. This is estimated to cost about $8 billion, which could go a long way toward bringing all HIPCs under our 2 percent ratio of debt service to GNP.[14] A subsequent real increase in ODA of 8 percent a year for 10 years would easily generate a cumulative total of more than $60 billion (which is actually far less ambitious than many European countries are currently proposing). This would cover the estimated $47 billion cost to bilaterals (table 5.6) for the extra countries that would be entitled to debt relief under our proposal. That would be true even if Indonesia, Nigeria, and Pakistan were to be offered those terms and accept them. That increase would also permit the augmentation of the trust funds that have been established to reimburse IDA and the regional development banks for the debt relief that they extend, bringing all the multilateral development banks into an expanded debt relief effort without damaging the interests of their other clients (estimated cost: $15 billion).[15]

As was noted above, these "cost" estimates exaggerate the accounting cost to donors, to the extent they have already written off the uncollectible portion. In the United States, for example, a good deal of bilateral debt owed by poor countries was accounted for as a loss throughout the 1990s, so that the actual legislative authorizations for debt reduction in 2000 were much smaller than the face value of such a reduction.

Such an increase would also give industrial countries the moral right to ask upper-middle-income countries to accept higher interest charges on their loans from the multilaterals, thus generating possible additional resources of about $4 billion over 10 years. Though the amount is small, this approach has the advantage of involving the upper-middle-income countries as donors in the international community, beginning to eliminate what is becoming an increasingly false distinction between donors and recipients.[16]

---

14. This $8 billion already pledged more than covers the bilateral component of our $10 billion estimate to bring all of the HIPCs under our threshold 2 percent ratio of debt service to GNP, thus providing some funds to go to the multilateral trust funds.

15. Indonesia represents 25 percent of the Asian Development Bank's (ADB's) total outstanding loan portfolio ($10-40 billion) and has $11 billion in IBRD outstanding loans. Table 5.6 shows that after Naples terms, Indonesia would still need a 50 percent reduction in its multilateral debt, which would mean a $5 billion hit for both the ADB and IBRD. In this context, donors should allow the ADB access to the HIPC Trust Fund to finance part of the ADB's debt reduction for Indonesia, and to ensure the financial integrity of the institution.

16. Note that Mexico and South Korea are already members of the OECD, and several of the upper-middle-income borrowers in Eastern Europe are hoping to join the European Union.

Figure 5.2 Authors' proposals

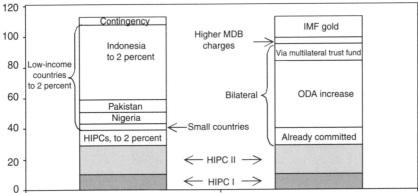

billions of dollars, NPV

MDB = multilateral development bank
NPV = net present value

Figure 5.2 summarizes our financing proposal. The right-hand bar shows HIPC I and II, the bilateral share (about $70 billion—$11 billion of which has already been pledged via complete cancellation for HIPCs and Pakistan's Paris Club deal in December 2001, plus about $59 billion that would finance additional bilateral cancellation and funding of the multilateral trust funds), higher financing from multilateral development bank charges ($4 billion over 10 years), and use of IMF gold ($9 billion for deepening and extending, plus the $5 billion estimate for the contingency facility).

If the donors do not agree to an increase in their ODA budgets for this debt reduction, then it would not be possible to make the three large countries—Indonesia, Nigeria, and Pakistan—eligible for debt reduction. We think eligibility should be offered to these countries. But if some of the donors refuse to sanction modest aid increases, then the resources for such an expanded program simply will not be present. One could still expand debt relief for the existing HIPCs by adding the 2 percent ceiling (estimated cost: $10 billion), adding the seven other small countries that would qualify for debt relief to the list of HIPCs (at an estimated cost of $4 billion), and putting in place the contingency facility we discussed. This program could be financed by the already pledged bilateral debt reduction plus IMF gold. In either event, it will be critical to monitor donor commitments to not squeeze existing aid programs, by holding donors to steady disbursements for future aid programs.[17]

---

17. Complete debt cancellation for the existing HIPCs would certainly threaten the level of ODA to non-HIPCs in the absence of higher ODA; the one circumstance in which it would be justifiable would be if it led to a high measure of additionality (and therefore did not squeeze non-HIPCs).

6

A New Aid Architecture

Debt relief is not a magic bullet for getting the development process in poor countries back on the rails. Indeed, elementary arithmetic tells us that—if the estimates of the cost of achieving the Millennium Development Goals are anywhere near the mark—even complete debt cancellation would not come near to sufficing. Any campaign directed to achieving those goals needs to focus on the issues of trade and aid, not just on debt—as does Bono's new campaign leading up to the 2002 Group of Eight summit.[1] There is also, of course, a whole agenda of domestic reforms that developing countries themselves need to pursue, spanning governance, macroeconomic discipline, the institutional infrastructure of a market economy, public expenditure on basic social services, and other priorities, as emphasized in the Monterrey consensus.[2] But this is not the place to explore that agenda.

In this chapter, we turn to the issue of how development assistance might be reformed to provide a more propitious financial environment for the poorest countries and to make sure that debt problems do not recur. We argue that a "new aid architecture" implies both fundamental reform in the way aid is delivered and a substantial increase in the volume of aid to the world's poorest countries for the next decade and beyond. Fundamental reform entails creating new incentives not only for recipients but for donors as well to focus on and be accountable for their perfor-

---

1. For a similar view, see also Serieux (2001).

2. We refer here to the United Nations conference on Financing for Development, held in Monterrey, Mexico, as this book went to publication in March 2002.

mance. That is the key to making the aid process more effective and ultimately to sustaining the necessary increase in aid flows.

We begin by discussing two incremental changes in the aid architecture, in HIPC procedures, and in the composition of aid between concessional loans and grants. We then turn to recommendations to build in incentives for more donor efficiency, selectivity, and additional aid in the future. The most important proposal is that the donor community move toward a "common pool" approach: to create a clear framework with incentives for both donor selectivity and recipient-country ownership of their development strategy.

The HIPC Procedure

The design of the enhanced HIPC Initiative is a first but modest step in building a new architecture. The idea is to make sure that money released from debt service actually gets devoted to basic social programs or is otherwise deployed to reduce poverty, as well as to ensure that this happens in a way that is chosen by the country itself. To reach the HIPC completion point where its debt stock is reduced, a country has to develop a Poverty Reduction Strategy Paper, in consultation with its own population, that lays out a national strategy to promote development and thus reduce poverty (see box 6.1).

The PRSP represents a new version of traditional conditionality in two senses: because the focus is on poverty reduction rather than structural adjustment (privatization, trade liberalization, etc.), and because donors hope that greater citizen participation will result in political "ownership" of the strategy and thus more sustained and effective implementation. The approach is based on experience in Uganda, which went through a 5-year participatory process that culminated in agreement on a Poverty Eradication Action Plan in 1997 (Mijumbi 2001). Because it is recognized that a truly participatory process is bound to take time, though it is urgent to provide highly indebted countries with relief, a country is allowed to obtain debt-service relief on an interim basis at a "decision point." This requires an interim PRSP, which covers much the same ground as a full PRSP but without the same elaborate requirements for public participation. The intent is nonetheless that the country should "own" the strategy.

Announcement of the requirements for the PRSP process provoked a fair amount of cynicism on the part of development professionals. Many recalled that (for example) Letters of Intent to the IMF and Letters of Development Policy to the World Bank are also supposed to be documents produced by the borrowing government, but that in practice they have long been written by IMF and World Bank staffers and presented to the would-be borrowing government to sign. In addition, concern was raised that the emphasis on poverty reduction via increases in social expendi-

Box 6.1 The PRSP challenge: Avoiding business as usual

The Poverty Reduction Strategy Papers, announced in 1999 as part of the enhanced HIPC Initiative, were hailed by the World Bank and IMF as a way both to address the contentious issue of conditionality versus ownership and to ensure that the proceeds from debt relief were spent to benefit the poor—especially by increasing education and health budgets. The PRSP envisaged a process whereby governments (aided by World Bank staff) would convene extensive consultations with civil society and nongovernmental actors, and prepare holistic, country-owned strategies that would form the basis for both HIPC and future donor assistance. One complaint in some countries is that parliaments have been largely bypassed in the process of popular consultation.

Unfortunately, there is an inherent tension between the focus on participation and the connection between the PRSP and release of HIPC debt relief proceeds. the second representing a form of donor-mandated conditionality that hinders the first. Though few argue that increased spending on education and health is a bad idea, many Southern NGO and civil society advocates caution not to confuse the preset goals of the PRSP process with country ownership. In May 2001, a group of 39 regional networks in 15 African countries argued that the PRSP is simply "window dressing" (Ranis and Stewart 2001).

Further, the long list of hoops that countries need to jump through to have a PRSP approved by the World Bank and IMF (and thus receive the proceeds of debt relief) has forced countries to sacrifice a participatory approach in the face of time constraints. Indeed, the detail and breadth demanded of the PRSP (detailed in Easterly 2001) has, to date, been beyond the capacity of nearly all of the HIPCs.

As of this writing, the World Bank and IMF had approved PRSPs from only four countries (Bolivia, Mozambique, Tanzania, and Uganda). It was to enable countries to start gaining the benefits of debt relief before they were able to complete the requisite participatory process for a full PRSP that Interim PRSPs were authorized as a sufficient condition for reaching the HIPC decision point. An Interim PRSP must cover the same ground, but it does not carry the same obligations for public participation in preparation.

Another danger is that PRSPs are not adequately addressing the task of monitoring, and that even if countries buy into the new donor conditionality, it will be impossible to tell where the proceeds of debt relief are really going. The World Bank and IMF (2001a) found that only two of the HIPCs will have the capacity to track spending related to debt relief transactions within the next year.

tures was primarily a donor-owned view, and would not necessarily be the optimal path for a country to attain sustainable growth and thus sustainable reductions in poverty.[3]

Why, then, should we expect PRSPs to be a step in the right direction? A possible answer is that the Bretton Woods institutions either have learned about the importance of country ownership and public participation or they finally believe their own propaganda about their importance. Another possibility is that the requirement for public participation makes it far more likely that countries will develop pro-poor policies and pro-

---

3. Addison and Rahman (2001); Burnside and Fanizza (2001).

grams and that vested interest groups will find it far more difficult to get away with business as usual. This applies to the preference of many HIPC governments for ignoring their own civil societies, and even parliaments, as well as the relationship between the World Bank and IMF and the countries involved.

In any event, some observers of early PRSP processes have concluded that the exercise is not just a charade, but is encouraging a degree of public involvement and a depth of citizen involvement and national ownership that were lacking in the past. For example, a Bread for the World case study on Zambia lauds the "unprecedented citizen participation in economic policy making" that the I-PRSP galvanized (McCarthy 2001). Booth (2001) is also fairly positive. Other observers are skeptical, raising the legitimate concern that citizen participation via a handful of public forums does not really embed the policy process within functioning institutions and may forestall rather than enhance real democratic politics— that is, the empowered legislature and regular free and fair elections that bring substantial accountability and ownership.[4]

Still, on the whole, we are inclined to the view that the PRSP process, imperfect as it may be, can make a difference, and if subsequent evidence confirms this, it is a gain not to be squandered. However, we see no need to delay debt-stock relief for years after a country has reached its decision point until a participatory PRSP has been completed. The decision point itself is conditional on a country's satisfying the traditional requirement for an IMF program—a reasonably sound macroeconomic regime. There is something of a contradiction between the notion that a country and its citizens need to own the PRSP strategy if it is to be sustainable and the additional conditionality of completing a PRSP by a set date.

As was argued above, some of the benefits of debt relief, notably those of enhancing national ownership and reassuring the private sector, are dependent on reducing the overhang of debt stock, and are not yielded simply by reducing the flow of debt-service payments. And it has been reported that pressure to bring HIPCs to the completion point is already leading to a rush to finish PRSPs, undermining the very process of participation and creation of political ownership that the PRSP is meant to encourage.

Moreover, the additional delays and the requirement to meet certain "standards" in a PRSP[5] elide the point that the debt to be canceled is

---

4. Marshall (2001) is skeptical about PRSPs. See also Van de Walle (2001).

5. World Bank staff have produced guidelines and recommendations for PRSPs, which are laid out in a 1,000-page sourcebook, covering such details as how to do household surveys, organize participatory processes, and design social service delivery mechanisms. (On the World Bank's mission creep, see Einhorn 2001). Of greater concern may be that PRSP conditions will work less well than traditional conditions because they apply to the political process, making them less realistic than ones on economic policy. It is difficult to imagine success in imposing democracy, as desirable as that might be.

Table 6.1 Continued aid dependence of post-completion point HIPCs

Country	Net official transfers (1997-99 annual average)	Debt service relief (2000-04 annual average)
Bolivia	482.3	125.8
Mozambique	926.3	119.3
Tanzania	907.0	77.0[a]
Uganda	647.0	50.8

a. Tanzania's completion point document is not yet publicly available. Therefore, this estimate relies on data from Tanzania's decision point document.

Source: World Bank Global Development Finance CD-ROM, 2001, and HIPC completion point documents.

fundamentally uncollectible—and thus seem to liberate donors and official creditors from recognizing and reforming whatever procedures or incentives led to the problem in the first place. If the donors were unlikely ever again to have the leverage needed to persuade these countries to go through the PRSP process, then it would make sense to delay the completion point in the interest of maintaining that leverage. But in fact there is no need for such leverage. On the contrary, all the existing HIPCs (though admittedly not all the additional candidates we have suggested) are heavily aid dependent and will remain so after debt reduction, even after the deeper debt reduction recommended above.

The reductions are in fact small relative to recent aid inflows. Table 6.1 displays the annual projected savings in debt service as a result of HIPC debt reductions and average annual net transfers in recent years for the four countries that have reached the HIPC completion point. In Uganda, the debt-service relief provided by the HIPC Initiative is only 8 percent of net official transfers. Recall also (at the end of chapter 3) that of our rough estimate of $25 billion a year in donor spending for the 42 HIPCs to achieve the Millennium Development Goals, our estimate of annual debt-service savings for those 42 countries (were all to reach the HIPC completion point) is a mere $4.2 billion a year.

If the donors announce that as from year 200x they are going to require that the Consultative Group be presented with a PRSP or else a country must expect aid commitments to be severely cut back, they will have ample pressure to ensure that the PRSP process continues to be taken seriously and continuing incentives for improving policies and building sound institutions. In other words, this consideration really does not provide a convincing case for delaying the full benefits of assured debt reduction. And it undermines the very notion of ownership.

Accordingly, we recommend the consolidation of the decision point and completion point. We recognize that this puts us in the paradoxical position of advocating aid selectivity, but only after a process of relatively nonselective debt cancellation (based only on macroeconomic stability but not an apparent dedication to a poverty strategy). Here is a case, however, where consistency in fact is nonsensical.

Grants, Not Just Loans

In a speech at the World Bank on 17 July 2001, US President George Bush suggested that IDA should convert about half its lending into grants. In this proposal, he echoed one of the few unanimous recommendations of the Meltzer Commission (2000). We strongly endorse this proposal, and we believe its endorsement by all the shareholders of the World Bank would clarify that for the poorest countries, where institutions are weak, disease burdens are high, geography is unpropitious, and civil conflicts and exogenous shocks frequently create havoc, it is perverse to demand repayment. Large resource transfers to countries where good leadership is committed to change will be necessary for a substantial period. A move to grants would also reflect official creditors' recognition that there was too much lending with too little selectivity in the past.

There are two principal arguments against IDA providing grants, but neither of them strikes us as any longer compelling. The first is based on incentive effects. The fear was that grants would be treated as easy come, easy go; loans, in contrast, were supposed to motivate recipients to use the resources well, for programs that encourage private-sector growth, yield increased tax revenue, or to build up human capital and strengthen institutions. But the evidence of the past 20 years is that this incentive effect does not necessarily provide sufficient discipline to restrain irresponsible borrowing. Governments are often prepared to accept loans without thought of the burden it will impose on future governments and future taxpayers. Moreover, nowadays a much larger proportion of aid goes to projects that are not expected to pay their way directly in financial terms (to schools and nutrition programs rather than power stations or dams).

The second argument was that IDA loans would in due course lead to a return flow of repayments that could then be recycled. It is surely good that in the 1960s South Korea received loans rather than grants, and is now repaying these and providing funds that IDA can lend to other countries that still have low incomes today. But even though 50 years were not enough to get development started everywhere, one has to be a real pessimist to expect the same need for supporting a large bloc of low-income countries in another 30 years time. And there is no point in having IDA loans repaid if, as became true in at least some HIPCs, this is financed by donor grants that are then not used for development investments.

The Europeans have resisted the Bush proposal in the run-up to the Monterrey Conference on Financing for Development, arguing for only limited use of IDA funds for grants.[6] They have spoken as though the loss of reflows to IDA was going to result in an equivalent reduction in the flow of financial resources to poor countries. This is not so. Most of the reduction in the reflow will be the counterpart to a reduced need to pay debt service and will therefore leave the countries just as well off as if they had paid the debt service out of money received in new IDA loans. Of course, there may be fewer jobs at the World Bank if IDA no longer has to make as many new loans to enable countries to pay it back, but we are surely not designing a job-creation program to benefit Washington.

The only benefit of receiving reflows would come from those countries that graduate from IDA and therefore repay money that can be recycled to other countries that are still poor. One has to ask whether there are likely to be enough countries in that category to outweigh the administrative costs of maintaining this recycling and the danger of pushing countries back into debt problems in the future. (And, diplomatically, it seems very silly of the Europeans to have picked a fight on this issue and thus diverted attention from the miserable US record on the volume of aid.)

The argument in favor of grants is of course that they will ensure that low-income countries do not again become overindebted, requiring a repeat of the HIPC exercise. The lack of reflows might increase the incentive for donors to insist on more selectivity on the part of IDA, so as to limit the use of large sums of grant money to countries truly able to absorb the resources effectively. For countries that are not performing well—for example, because they are run by crooks—IDA grants should be limited to much smaller sums designed to support policy dialogue, highly focused institutional reform, and so forth.

IDA grants, as is the case with loans, should still be made primarily to governments; policy dialogue and policy leverage with governments, especially regarding poverty strategies, is the comparative advantage of the World Bank's IDA. If country governments are not reliable or are simply unable to manage resources well, humanitarian, relief, training, and other institution-building programs would not go through IDA via governments but would be financed and managed by the United Nations specialized agencies, the bilaterals, and more and more by private sources, all of which have shown an ability to work with local NGOs.

Applying the principle of donor selectivity between the best-performing countries and the ones that are run by predatory governments is not very difficult. The problem comes in dealing appropriately with countries in the middle: ones with governments whose leaders mean well but are either following a misguided ideology (Tanzania under Julius Nyerere or

---

6. The debate as we went to publication was over specific amounts, with the United States proposing that 50 percent of IDA resources be in the form of grants, and the Europeans suggesting amounts in the range of 10 to 20 percent.

Zambia under Kenneth Kaunda come to mind) or else lack any competent administrative apparatus capable of putting their intentions into action. The problem also comes, practically speaking, in the constant stream of decisions that must be made about whether to enter strongly in support of a new government, and whether and when to withdraw major support. We turn to this issue of selectivity below; at this point, we simply note that in an environment where grant funding is disbursed on the basis of performance, it is likely to be easier to implement decisions about entry and withdrawal effectively.

Incremental Proposals to Increase Donor Accountability

We have emphasized that the donors and official creditors must take some responsibility for the buildup of unsustainable debt in the world's poorest countries. With the HIPC Initiative, they are taking some financial responsibility. But formalizing four new procedures would also contribute.

First, to create more visible, credible donor accountability, we recommend the modest additions to DAC reporting and changes in its accounting set out above (see box 4.1). Reporting the appropriate portions of official debt that is canceled as a loss would emphasize that at least some portion of the existing unsustainable debt of poor countries is truly uncollectible. Ending the practice of recording as ODA (uncollectible) interest arrears and cancellation of export credits would allow improved monitoring of official creditors' lending and of donors' overall commitments by development activists.

Second, we recommend that the PRGF be transferred from the IMF to the World Bank. Such a transfer would make the PRSP process, and the lending in support of it, the unambiguous responsibility of the World Bank.[7] The consolidation of the Poverty Reduction Support Credits already given by the World Bank with PRGF loans would presumably yield some administrative savings.

If one is going to consolidate in the interest of increasing accountability and efficiency, then clearly the World Bank should be in charge. The purpose of the PRGF is poverty reduction, which is the raison d'être of

---

7. Already there are differences in approach between the two institutions, reducing the accountability of either one. E.g., the IMF has approved many more interim PRSPs in order to resume lending; the World Bank, perhaps because it has the option of project lending independent of an approved PRSP, has not approved more than one or two Poverty Reduction Support Credits.

the World Bank. The IMF argues that its professional concern is macroeconomic policy and that disciplined macro policies are necessary for poverty reduction to have a chance, which is a viewpoint we endorse. However, an appropriate IMF role in ensuring macroeconomic discipline could perfectly well be secured by having the IMF monitor the macroeconomic component of each country's strategy. Macroeconomics is only one dimension, albeit an important one, that a country needs to get roughly right if it is to have a chance to grow rapidly and equitably, and all the other relevant issues except possibly the financial sector—from governance to the social sector—are primarily World Bank responsibilities. Hence it would be altogether more logical to conduct PRGF lending out of the bank.

It would be desirable for the IMF to transfer all those PRGF assets that remain after debt relief along the lines discussed above to the World Bank. The total assets of the PRGF at the moment, including its outstanding loans to HIPCs and other poor countries, amount to about $10 billion. Because about 70 percent of the loans are to HIPCs, and there will be more to other countries to which we suggested extending HIPC status, the assets coming with the HIPC Initiative would be fairly modest.

Third, we suggest that the donors, as shareholders in the World Bank and the regional development banks, instruct those institutions to encourage and be prepared to finance any initiative of borrowing countries to seek independent credit counseling. With independent advice, borrowers might resist the temptation to seek donor-guaranteed export credits for the purchase of unnecessarily expensive goods embodying inappropriate technology, as in the notorious case of the Tanzanian purchase of British radar in December 2001.

Fourth, the OECD's Development Assistance Committee might add to its mandate the development of principles on appropriate donor conduct, and then seek procedures to monitor how well donors measure up to those principles. One idea is for the donors' trade association, the DAC, to enlist an equivalent body representing the aid recipients. Although the administrative systems of aid recipients are already overstretched, so that one would not want to see them devoting the effort that would be needed to create a full equivalent to the DAC, it should be easy for the Group of 24 (say) to organize an annual discussion on these issues in the course of one of its regular meetings. A small number of the members could then be asked to convey the sense of the meeting to the donors' representatives in the DAC, allowing donors and aid recipients to discuss the issues in a less asymmetrical framework than arises in the typical one-on-one or Consultative Group setting. That could be complimented by the DAC's financing, on a pilot basis, borrowers' monitoring of the donors within their countries. For example, Ghana might receive a DAC grant to manage a 2-year program of in-country reporting on the costs and benefits of donor activities.

Donor Incentives for Selectivity

The reason for widespread skepticism about the effectiveness of aid is that so much of it has been given for the wrong reasons, notably to support diplomatic, strategic, or commercial goals rather than developmental ones. At its worst, aid has sometimes been used to support predatory governments run by tyrants interested primarily in looting the economy or building up their foreign bank accounts rather than in what happens to their citizens. In the past, even such villains often continued to receive foreign aid regardless of their failings, sometimes because of strategic concerns and sometimes because of a desire to preserve the fiction that debt was being serviced. A new aid architecture needs to make sure that aid is instead directed to where it can be most effectively used in curbing poverty by promoting economic and human development.

We have argued that debt relief can help in securing this reorientation, by getting rid of the pressure to lend so as to maintain debt service, and thus allowing for greater future selectivity by donors. But a new emphasis on selectivity also means the donor community holding itself to a standard of directing aid overwhelmingly to those countries meeting the twin criteria of the prevalence of poverty and the presence of policies that will make an effective assault on poverty.

Making the concept of selectivity operational is not straightforward (see box 6.2). What steps might take the donor community in the right direction?

The World Bank, in its IDA lending, has already shown a modest but important ability to direct more lending to countries that are "performing" better under its "performance-based allocation system." One way of improving the donors' ability to be selective would be to improve the information base available to them. In particular, it would be possible for the World Bank to publish the full details of the annual Country Policy and Institutional Assessment that it undertakes on all of its IDA borrowing members.

This information would enable donors to assess whether they believe that the numbers generated in the course of this exercise deserve to be taken seriously. To the extent that their judgment is indeed positive, it would then provide donors with the equivalent of an annual credit rating, one tailored to assessing the extent to which a country can be expected to profit from the use of external resources. Making the basis for the annual country index publicly available would also allow for the ongoing scholarly and public scrutiny from which country policymakers, citizens, and local and foreign investors, as well as donors, could benefit.

In addition, thought could be given to keying the index of country performance not to the relative allocation of IDA resources across countries but to the absolute amounts. That would imply that if more countries become more capable of using resources well, the total amount of aid

Box 6.2   Assessing country performance: Selectivity using what measures?

We have emphasized in this book that donors ought to be more *selective* across countries with their aid, that is, channel more resources to countries most in need and best able to use the resources well. The evidence has accumulated that linking aid to fulfillment of donor-specified conditions has not worked. This has not necessarily been because the conditions made no sense (though some argue that is also the case), but because the reforms they demanded need to be autonomously driven, or "owned," by the societies benefiting from the aid transfers to be implemented effectively and sustained (Collier 2000; Ellerman 2001).

This is particularly true for reforms that cannot be implemented with the stroke of a pen (e.g., tariff cutting), but require the understanding and commitment of politicians, bureaucrats, customs officials, and others (e.g., customs reforms, property rights, strengthening an independent judiciary).[1] In other words, bribing governments or societies into good behavior (conditions as carrots) does not work, nor does refusing to disburse loans when governments fail to comply with conditions (conditions as sticks).

Conversely, there is also plenty of evidence that aid does work when governments are already in the process of developing the policies and institutions likely to induce long-run growth and poverty reduction. Then it makes sense for donors to commit large amounts of resources—to enable governments to accelerate the process, lock it in politically, and raise welfare more quickly. (Such a process of "rewards" might also help citizens in countries not so committed whose governments are not being supported to mobilize in favor of the same changes.)

But what are reasonable measures of a government in a particular country being "in the process" described (all too vaguely) above? Consider three familiar ones. The first is a macroeconomic policy mix that sufficiently minimizes inflation. There may be controversy about the optimal mix of monetary and fiscal policy and the limits of austerity in bad times. Certainly no country needs to run a budget surplus year after year; countercyclical deficits and deficits financed by manageable debt make sense. But no one resists anymore the need to take the measures necessary to prevent inflation rising above 10 percent, recognizing the difficulties of containing further increases and the burden imposed by inflation on the poor.

The second measure is a minimally "liberal" state, that is, one not so heavily engaged in productive and financial activities that emergence of a competitive, reasonably efficient economy is unlikely. There is plenty of controversy on the minimum depth and the right sequencing of the changes implied for some countries—privatization, financial-sector reform, trade liberalization. But no one argues anymore in favor of a state-managed, Soviet-style economy.

The third measure is a minimally corrupt state. Transparent budgets, checks on executive discretion, rule of law, respect for human rights including the rights of women, and the accompanying political and social institutions (a free press, contestable elections, etc.). Some would extend this farther, to include participation of citizens in political and community life, an active civil society of nongovernmental organizations, unions, faith communities, and even a particular form of liberal (Western) democracy.

---

1. Rodrik (2000) emphasizes this point.

(box continues next page)

Box 6.2 Assessing country performance: Selectivity using what measures? *(continued)*

The traditional conditionality of the IMF and the multilateral development banks has concentrated on the first two economic issues above. Even today, the decision point for eligible HIPCs is conditional on a minimum period of demonstrated macroeconomic stability, sufficient for the IMF to be satisfied. We have argued in the text for collapsing decision and completion points. That implies a nonselective approach for debt cancellation, except for the minimal macroeconomic conditionality. (It also implies eligibility of some postconflict countries for debt cancellation sooner than otherwise.)

We have also emphasized that the needs of the debtor countries for more post-HIPC transfers are huge. Debt cancellation will only reduce their current obligations by about 10 percent of the estimated costs to them of meeting the Millennium Development Goals. With our proposed debt-cancellation package, the poorest countries' debt will itself be sustainable. They will then be in a position to get "into the process" set out above, and donors ought to be in a position to support them—or not, depending on their performance.

We believe that as a community and in close partnership with borrowing and debtor countries, donors ought to develop and fine-tune a clear set of benchmarks for a country being adequately in that elusive process. Our own inclination would be to put much more emphasis on performance on the measures of minimal corruption, or "governance." A minimum level of adequate governance might reasonably be made a precondition for new large transfers, independent of other measures, given the evidence that high levels of corruption inhibit growth and hurt the poor.

In any event, any such measures would need to be made more concrete and transparent. And even then, much would have to be left to the ongoing judgment of each donor.[2] The development of countries and people is not, after all, without risks—any more than is the development of defense missiles or new software businesses.

The people living in countries that do not meet the minimum thresholds for selectivity need not be altogether abandoned. Support for nongovernmental groups working to protect the environment, provide social services, and fight for democracy still makes sense, as does humanitarian and relief work with victims of repressive governments and civil conflicts. But large loans and grants to and through governments should be confined to countries that meet minimum criteria.

---

2. The Country Policy and Institutional Assessment (CPIA) index of the World Bank does include assessment of governance arrangements, and we understand there is now consideration of giving governance greater weight in the overall index. But, as was noted, the country-by-country basis for the CPIA is not public.

would rise. It would also mean that were countries unable to absorb resources for one or more years, IDA resources could be used for additional financing of such global public goods as tropical agricultural research or the development of vaccines against infectious diseases.

Exploiting Multilateralism: The Common Pool

A second mechanism for donor self-regulation implies a more ambitious change in the way official aid is delivered. We argued in chapter 4 that there are various efficiency reasons for preferring debt relief to more ODA: ownership, transaction costs, fungibility, eliminating tied aid, and encouraging private investment. All those reasons except the last can also be cited in support of a proposal for reforming the process for granting aid called the *common pool proposal*. Note that a common pool would still allow different donors to give different amounts in different countries, allowing donors to back those countries where they like the program best.

The common pool idea was developed by Kanbur and Sandler (1999). They suggest that each aid recipient should go through a PRSP-like process to elaborate on its own development strategy, programs, and projects—primarily in consultation with its own population but also in a dialogue with donors. It would then present the plans to its donors, which would, to the extent that the plans meet with their favor, put unrestricted financing into a common pool of development assistance. This, together with the government's own resources, would finance the overall development strategy of the country in question.

The level of financing from each donor would depend on its assessment of both the strategy and the recipient country's ability to implement the strategy and monitor progress and expenditures. Donors' views would be made known to the country during the dialogue leading up to the financing decision, but earmarking of this or that donor's funds for this or that item, or donor monitoring and control of specific projects or programs, would not be permitted.

The international community has already moved toward this proposal by adopting the World Bank's Comprehensive Development Framework and the PRSP process. The recent statement by a dozen African heads of state adopting the New Partnership for African Development is also based fundamentally on the idea of a contract or partnership between donors and recipients, in which recipients ask donors to link the level of aid to recipients' performance in combating corruption, implementing the rule of law, and maintaining stable macroeconomic regimes.

This philosophy is also embedded in the agreed-on declaration of nations at the Monterrey Conference on Financing for Development. We suggest that the international community now make good on its own rhetoric by having all the bilateral donors channel their bilateral as well as multilateral assistance through recipient-country governments in this way. That would not only solve the nagging problem of poor donor coordination, it would place accountability for the selectivity with the donors, and for the success of the development program itself squarely where it belongs, with recipient-country governments.

Sovereign Debt: Building on the HIPC Initiative

One proposal of the debt campaigners does not seem to us to merit endorsement. This is the proposal mentioned in chapter 2 to set up an independent arbitration procedure, managed at the United Nations or another noncreditor agency, and including input from civil society groups, to handle a bankruptcy-like procedure for poor countries with unsustainable sovereign debt, including that owed to official international creditors and rich-country governments (Raffer 2001).

We agree that some sort of formal procedure for handling the debt of poor countries owed to official creditors does make sense.[8] But it would be pointless to force donors into debt relief that they were in a position to offset simply by cutting new transfers. It is unrealistic to think that donors would ever lock themselves into an arbitration proceeding that would coerce from them additional transfers, and we see no benefit in encouraging such an illusion.

In our view, the HIPC procedure itself represents an agreed-on bankruptcy-like procedure. It reflects the reality that official creditors have taken a serious measure of responsibility for their lending, which in retrospect has turned out to be unsustainable. We therefore believe that the most sensible and practical way to handle that debt is to build on the precedent set by the HIPC Initiative, by incorporating our proposals for ambitious but incremental reform recommended above.

---

8. The recent proposal of Anne Krueger of the IMF for a formal mechanism would apply to countries whose debt is primarily commercial, not official.

7

Conclusions

During the past several decades, a large number of the poorest countries in the world took on more debt than they were able to service except by obtaining ever more aid. A group of debt campaigners headed by Jubilee and with illustrious supporters like Bono and the pope led a campaign to cancel these debts, which they argued were unjust and were sabotaging the ability of those countries' governments to provide minimal social services to their citizens. The HIPC Initiative was the response of the G-7 and the international financial institutions (notably the IMF and World Bank) to that campaign. The first initiative was announced in 1996, and an enhanced version providing more, faster debt relief was agreed to in 1999.

The donor countries had good reasons to cancel some debt owed to them by the poorest countries, even without the political pressure of the Jubilee movement. In the poorest countries, including most of Africa, two decades of official lending, most of it at concessional rates, had failed to catalyze the increased growth and new economic activities needed to finance the existing debt and pull people out of poverty. In some of the HIPCs, donors were locked into defensive lending: endless rounds of rescheduling the debt and negotiating new grants and loans to help poor countries pay back old loans.

In this study, we have set out this background to what became the 1999 enhanced HIPC Initiative. Most HIPCs have had limited if any per capita growth during the past two decades. Poor growth (and the resulting unsustainable debt) were the outcome in some countries of incompetence, even thievery, and in others of unmanageable disease burdens, civil conflicts, lack of human capital and adequate infrastructure, and declines in the world prices of their limited export products. Much of the lending by Western governments was meant to address these constraints to growth. But even when well intentioned, it was often poorly channeled, reflecting Cold War politics rather than development objectives.

Among critics of the HIPC Initiative are some who think it is too big, too fast, and likely to "waste" more resources, and others convinced that, given the problems of the poorest countries, it is too small, too slow, and laden with the kind of IMF and World Bank "conditionalities" that they claim have not worked in the past.

Whether to Extend More Debt Relief

Against this background, we have argued that there are two compelling grounds for the international community to give more help to the HIPCs. More help is needed both to be reasonably sure that they will escape from debt unsustainability and also to give them a reasonable chance of achieving the Millennium Development Goals. But this positive answer does not necessarily imply that it makes sense to give more debt relief; we have argued that it is also necessary to ask whether debt relief (as opposed to bigger disbursements of new aid) is the right *way* to give additional help.

We have identified a number of factors that are relevant in making this choice. To begin with, the widespread concern that much of the debt is unjust, or odious, means that the cause of debt relief has gained significant political appeal, which gives hope that it can be a channel for bringing a net addition of real resources to the cause of development. This is important, because if there were no additionality then it would be other developing countries that would pay the bill for debt relief. We have traced the redistributive channels through which this can occur, including some that have not been acknowledged by all of the debt campaigners, such as the way in which a raid on the reserves of the multilateral development banks would increase their cost of borrowing, which would then get passed on to their other clients in the form of higher interest rates or lower new lending.

But we then noted that even if there were no additionality or redistributive effects at all—so that the volume of real resources going to these countries was totally unaffected—there are powerful reasons why debt relief might still be the right choice. In brief, the substitution of debt relief for aid disbursements can increase the efficiency of aid by increasing ownership of their development programs by poor countries, reducing transaction costs, increasing fungibility, eliminating tying, and reassuring the private sector that countries are going to be able to implement their plans. And debt relief can also free donors of the need for defensive lending, liberating them to put their new aid where they believe it can do the most good.

How to Extend the HIPC Initiative

The analysis leads us to conclude that it makes sense to extend the HIPC Initiative further, in three dimensions. First, we recommend deeper debt cancellation to eligible HIPCs where debt service still exceeds 2 percent of GNP. That will ensure that the burden on the countries' budgets remains manageable. It also means that no really poor country that makes a serious effort at getting its own citizens to pay taxes would have to use more than 10 percent of its tax revenue to pay debt service. The cost: $10 billion.

Second, we recommend expanding the HIPC Initiative to make eligible more low-income countries—including big ones like Indonesia, Nigeria, and Pakistan. It would be a mistake to concentrate what extra funds may be available for debt relief just on the existing HIPCs, because that would discriminate against the millions of comparably poor people in these other countries simply because they had better luck or better governments at some point in the past, or because they live in larger countries whose high absolute costs for debt relief the donors have been reluctant to face. The cost: $70 billion, including almost $50 billion for Indonesia.

Third, we recommend safeguarding countries (through a contingent facility at the IMF) for 10 years against being pushed back into unsustainable debt levels by circumstances beyond their control. Cost: unknown; we use $5 billion as illustrative because the current annual cost of the existing short-term contingency facility has been estimated at about $500 million.

Cost of the Extensions

The total cost of these extensions is thus between $30 and $80 billion. Most of the variation in this wide range depends on whether or not Indonesia is included, plus the unknown cost of the contingency facility.

A sizable portion of the costs should be financed by the mobilization of IMF gold, which could yield more than $20 billion. We propose that the IMF shareholders agree to mobilize gold to finance all the debts owed to the IMF, plus the cost of the contingency facility.

The remainder should be financed by an increase in donor contributions to foreign aid, partly through canceling bilateral debt, and partly by increased payments to the HIPC Trust Fund. We do not wish to see the MDBs emasculated by being forced to run down their reserves.

The case for making Indonesia eligible is strong: It has been pushed back into the ranks of low-income countries by the post-1997 crisis, it is highly indebted on every available measure, and there seem good reasons for believing that a lower debt burden would pay rapid dividends in revived growth and reduced poverty. Yet its inclusion is feasible only in the context of a major expansion of ODA (even if some of the bilateral debt has already been written down in accounting terms). Conversely, major expansion of debt relief in the absence of a corresponding increase in ODA (at minimum sustaining a steady outflow of new disbursements) would be pointless, because there would be too much robbing of Peter to pay Paul. In that sense, the debt campaign is and must be a campaign for more aid.

Toward a New Aid Architecture

But the case for more aid is unlikely to be successful without changes in the existing aid architecture—changes that would create greater incentives for donors to be accountable as well as for recipients to perform better. If one takes the optimistic view that the introduction of PRSPs is making a major difference in how aid is delivered—such as to make a reality of country ownership while strengthening the expectation that aid will be concentrated on those who will use it effectively—this has already started.

We have made a number of proposals—some no doubt controversial—for more transparency in the ODA accounts, for transferring the PRGF from the IMF to World Bank, for increased pressure on donors to channel aid selectively, and for expanding the scope of the aid that is provided under the umbrella of the PRSP to include bilateral aid (this would implement the common pool proposal). As always, aid is second best to trade: any campaign that aims to help poor countries needs to place their fair access to the markets of rich countries very high on its agenda.

By putting the issue of rich-country responsibility for helping the poor help themselves squarely back on the table, the debt campaigners have done an enormous service to the cause of development. Our analysis has linked debt relief to the even larger challenge of renewing and reforming the donors' aid architecture. With more and better aid and freer trade, there would indeed be real hope of reviving the drive for development and achieving the Millennium Development Goals.

Appendix A
Multilateral Institutions Participating in the HIPC Initiative

AfDB/AfDF	African Development Bank/African Development Fund
AMF	Arab Monetary Fund
ADB	Asian Development Bank
BADEA	Arab Bank for Economic Development in Africa
BCEAO	Banque Centrale des Etats d'Afrique de l'Ouest
BDEAC	Banque des Etats de l'Afrique Centrale
BOAD	West African Development Bank
CABEI	Central American Bank for Economic Integration
CAF	Corporación Andina de Fomento
CDB	Caribbean Development Bank
CMCF	Caricom Multilateral Clearing Facility
EADB	East African Development Bank
EU/EIB	European Union/European Investment Bank
ECOWAS	Fund for Cooperation, Compensation, and Development of the Economic Community of West African States
FADES	Arab Fund for Social and Economic Development
FEGECE	Conseil de l'Entente
FOCEM	Fondo Centroamericano de Estabilización Monetaria
FONPLATA	Fund for the Financial Development of the River Plate Basin
IDB	Inter-American Development Bank
IFAD	International Fund for Agricultural Development
IsDB	Islamic Development Bank
NDF	Nordic Development Fund
NIB	Nordic Investment Bank
OPEC Fund	Organization of Petroleum Exporting Countries Fund for International Development
PTA Bank	Eastern and Southern African Trade and Development Bank

Appendix B
Countries Classified by Income

Low-income countries

Afghanistan
Angola
Armenia
Azerbaijan
Bangladesh
Benin
Burkina Faso
Burundi
Cambodia
Cameroon
Central African
  Republic
Chad
Congo, Democratic
  Republic of
Congo, Republic of
Côte d'Ivoire
Eritrea
Ethiopia
Gambia
Ghana

Guinea
Guinea-Bissau
Guyana
Haiti
India
Indonesia
Kenya
North Korea
Kyrgyzstan
Lao PDR
Lesotho
Liberia
Madagascar
Malawi
Mali
Mauritania
Moldova
Mongolia
Mozambique
Myanmar
Nepal

Nicaragua
Niger
Nigeria
Pakistan
Rwanda
São Tomé and Principe
Senegal
Sierra Leone
Somalia
Sudan
Tajikistan
Tanzania
Togo
Uganda
Ukraine
Uzbekistan
Vietnam
Yemen
Zambia
Zimbabwe

Lower-middle-income economies

Albania
Algeria
Belarus
Bolivia
Bosnia and
    Herzegovina
Bulgaria
China
Colombia
Cuba
Dominican Republic
Ecuador
Egypt
El Salvador

Georgia
Guatemala
Honduras
Iran
Iraq
Jamaica
Jordan
Kazakhstan
Latvia
Lithuania
Macedonia
Morocco
Namibia
Papua New Guinea

Paraguay
Peru
Philippines
Romania
Russia
Sri Lanka
Swaziland
Syria
Thailand
Tunisia
Turkmenistan
West Bank and Gaza
Yugoslavia
    (Serbia-Montenegro)

Upper-middle-income countries

Argentina
Botswana
Brazil
Chile
Costa Rica
Croatia
Czech Republic
Estonia
Hungary

Lebanon
Libya
Malaysia
Mauritius
Mexico
Oman
Panama
Poland

Puerto Rico
Saudi Arabia
Slovak Republic
South Africa
South Korea
Turkey
Uruguay
Venezuela

High-income economies

Australia
Austria
Belgium
Canada
Denmark
Finland
France
Germany
Greece

Hong Kong
Ireland
Israel
Italy
Japan
Kuwait
Netherlands
New Zealand
Norway

Portugal
Singapore
Slovenia
Spain
Sweden
Switzerland
United Arab Emirates
United Kingdom
United States

Source: World Bank, *Global Development Finance* CD-ROM, 2001.

Appendix C
Odious Debt

In this appendix, we explore one of the more persuasive arguments for debt relief: the injustice of requiring citizens of poor countries to pay back debts that were used for purposes never intended to benefit them—and that they did not agree to in any democratic process—but were acquired by corrupt or otherwise illegitimate governments. We set the stage with a rough estimate of the magnitude of the problem, and then turn to five country case studies. We examine the experiences of the Democratic Republic of Congo (the former Zaire), Kenya, Nicaragua, Pakistan, and Uganda (four HIPCs and one country that some people have argued ought to be a HIPC). For each case, we report standard debt data and discuss what evidence we could find about factors likely to reflect odious debt, such as wealth accumulation by leading political figures, largely unproductive public investment or other spending, and capital flight.

Table C.1 shows the total share of annual commitments made by the international community during the past three decades to HIPCs that, in the year of the commitment, were ranked not free, corrupt, or both not free and corrupt in one or another of the widely known international indices. The first measure, and index of political and civil freedom, comes from Freedom House (available for the period 1972-99); countries are categorized free, partly free, or not free. The second measure, a corruption index, is from the *International Country Risk Guide* (available for the period 1982-95) and categorized on a scale of 0 to 6.

Using the first index, of the nearly $140 billion of loans committed to HIPCs between 1972 and 1999, about 60 percent has gone to countries considered not free in the year they received the commitment. Using both

Table C.1 Odious debt: Commitments to countries considered "Not Free" and "Corrupt" (billions of dollars)

Commitments	Amount
To HIPCs, 1972-99[a]	139.2
To governments rated not free (NF)[b]	82.6 (59 percent)
To HIPCs, 1982-95[c]	85.6
Amount committed to countries scoring 0-3 on corruption scale[d]	57.1 (67 percent)
Amount committed to NF governments with 0-3 corruption scores	28.6 (33 percent)

a. Data for the 31 countries for which Freedom House data are available.

b. Freedom House rankings are based on annual surveys of political and civil liberties from 1972 to 1999. Countries are labeled as free, partly free, and not free according to these rankings.

c. Data for the 24 countries where both Freedom House and ICRG data are available.

d. The *International Country Risk Guide* (ICRG) corruption index is compiled by a private investment risk service and is scored on a scale of 0-6. The index is available from 1982 to 1995.

Sources: Commitments are from all creditors, World Bank, *Global Development Finance* CD-ROM, 2001.

indices, of the commitments made to countries between 1982 and 1995, 33 percent went to countries ranked both not free and corrupt (scores of 0-3). Of course, some of these commitments were not fully disbursed, but the commitments themselves signal the willingness of international donors to engage in these environments.

It is, in short, hard to deny that at least some of the debt of these countries could be considered odious. The case studies bring us to the same conclusion. As we discuss above in the text, however, it is difficult to make operational in any way the concept of odious debt—for example, in judging after the fact what amount of debt relief makes sense.

Democratic Republic of Congo (Zaire)

The Democratic Republic of Congo (DRC) is a large resource-dependent country that has been ravaged by recession, dictatorship, and civil strife for the past three decades. It is perhaps the clearest case of a government accumulating debt for odious purposes and for nondevelopment objectives. From 1965 to 1997, under the dictatorship of President Joseph Desire Mobutu, the Zairian government received more than $4.5 billion in strate-

Table C.2 Resource flows and other indicators for the Democratic Republic of Congo (Zaire), 1970-99 (millions of constant 1995 dollars, annual)

Flow or indicator	1970-79	1980-84	1985-89	1990-94	1995-99	Total, 1980-99
Debt outstanding	5,736	5,157	8,867	9,629	8,901	8,141 (average)
Disbursements	824	363	392	163	1	4,596
Bilateral	186	158	108	24	1	1,454
Multilateral	61	84	265	139	0	2,440
Private	576	121	19	1	0	701
Total debt service	240	308	263	65	0	3,182
Debt transfers	583	55	129	98	1	1,414
Grants	343	282	330	360	168	5,695
Total net transfers	926	336	459	458	169	7,109
Debt to GNP	19	39	88	116	167	n.a.
Debt to exports	131	219	288	575	552	n.a.
Debt service paid to GNP	1	2	3	1	0	n.a.
Capital flight[a]	712	674	156	490	−349[b]	13,099 (1970-96)
Fortune amassed by dictator	n.a.	n.a.	n.a.	n.a.	n.a.	4,000-5,000[c]
Freedom House ranking	Not free	Not free	Not free	Not free	Not free	
Corruption ranking (0-6)[d]		0	0	0		

n.a. = not applicable

a. Capital flight data from Boyce and Ndikumana (2001). Capital flight data for other countries are from Schneider (2001), who does not include Democratic Republic of Congo in her dataset.

b. 1995-96 only.

c. Estimates vary (see below).

d. 0 = most corrupt. Data are from 1982 to 1995.

Source: World Bank Global Development Finance CD-ROM, 2001, unless otherwise noted.

gically motivated aid from Western governments and aid agencies (table C.2).

Recognizing Zaire as a linchpin of the Cold War, Western governments, as well as the IMF and World Bank, committed this financing to the Mobutu regime despite evidence that he had installed an essentially kleptocratic state where rampant corruption and lawlessness made development nearly impossible. Evidence suggests that little if any of this money went to increase government expenditure for development purposes. In 1965, per capita income in the DRC was $340; by 1997, it had collapsed to $113, making the DRC the second poorest country in the world.

Accumulation of Congolese Debt

With its independence in 1960, the DRC was thrown into a state of chaos, until Mobutu consolidated power in a bloodless coup in 1965. For the next decade, Zaire's[1] economy performed well, benefiting from favorable oil prices, and received large amounts of financing on commercial terms from abroad. In 1973, for example, total disbursements (new loans plus grants) to Zaire were more than $1 billion, mostly from private creditors. During this period, the United States also invested significantly in Zaire to develop industrial capacity and infrastructure, including for a large electrical power-line project.

In the mid-1970s, Zaire's economy faltered with the first international oil shock, declining terms of trade (a 40 percent drop in copper prices in 1975), and the accumulation of debt without a corresponding buildup of productive assets. In 1973, Mobutu nationalized all major economic activities, and in 1974 Zaire went into arrears, first with its private creditors and then with official creditors as well. By 1975, Zaire's stock of debt was about $3.7 billion, already 160 percent of exports. In 1975, Zaire was already a heavily indebted and poor country by today's standards.

The international community continued to lend to Zaire despite its arrears status, and despite increasing worries about the political and human rights abuses of the Mobutu regime. In 1979, arrears for the first time reached $1 billion, and Mobutu agreed to a standby arrangement with the IMF, rescheduling bilateral and commercial debt so as to reduce arrears to less than $100 million. Then, between 1980 and 1982, Zaire borrowed heavily again, receiving $2.3 billion in new gross disbursements (including grants). The bulk of this new lending came from official bilateral sources, as private creditors pulled out of Zaire. Again, there is little evidence that any of this money was used for development purposes. With another major terms-of-trade erosion in the early 1980s, Zaire fell into recession and by 1983 its arrears had climbed back to $830 million. Transfers from the international community fell as well, reaching a low of $54 million in 1985.

In the second half of the 1980s, the composition of financing to Zaire changed again, as bilateral creditors backed off from providing new loans, and the IMF and World Bank filled the gap. In 1987, Zaire received support from the Structural Adjustment Facility, and the World Bank released the first tranche of a structural adjustment credit of $150 million. Despite little progress toward the stated goals of the country's structural adjustment program, the World Bank gave the Zairian government the benefit of the doubt, and it released the second tranche in 1989. By early 1990, it became clear that Mobutu had little interest in adhering to the program, and he was cut off from all international financing.

In 1991, Zaire's debt reached it highest point, at nearly $10 billion. The Mobutu regime stopped servicing its debt altogether, and since 1992 has been a rogue debtor to the international community. Zaire has been in

---

1. Mobutu changed the name of the Democratic Republic of Congo to Zaire in 1967.

nonaccrual status to the World Bank since November 1993. In 1996, the civil war intensified in Zaire, and in May 1997 Mobutu fled the country as the rebel coalition named the Alliance of Democratic Forces for the Liberation of Congo (ADFLC) took control. The country has since been embroiled in a bitter civil war. The DRC is one of the 42 countries that is in principle eligible for the enhanced HIPC program, but its ongoing conflict status and massive arrears make it unlikely to benefit any time soon.

Odious Nature of Congolese Debt

The debt amassed under the Mobutu regime seems to meet all of the criteria of odious debt. First, Mobutu's personal fortune leaves little doubt where much of the failed development assistance financing ended up. An investigation by the *Financial Times* estimated his personal wealth at $4 billion (*Financial Times*, 12 May 1997, A1). The figure dropped subsequently because Mobutu was financing the war against rebel factions. Another source (*Washington Post*, 18 April 1997, "Mobutu's Fall from Riches to Rags," A22) notes World Bank documents estimating that Mobutu extracted about $400 million a year from Zaire's copper and cobalt exports during the 1980s, and that this was only one component of his embezzlement of Zairian resources. The same source quotes rebels in 1997 claiming that Mobutu's holdings in Switzerland alone were $4-5 billion. Assuming $4 billion as a conservative estimate,[2] Mobutu's fortune was equivalent to about half of the DRC's total outstanding debt in 1997 and 28 percent of its GNP.

Mobutu's fortune reflected his theft of natural resources and excessive borrowing, most of which found its way into capital flight. Boyce and Ndikumana (2001) estimate the total capital flight from the DRC during the period 1970-96 as greater than the size of the accumulated stock of debt during this period. Capital flight was especially high during periods of crisis, reaching nearly $2 billion in 1973-74, and again jumping to $2 billion in 1978 and $1 billion in 1990. Overall, capital flight averaged 3.2 percent of GDP annually (for comparison, spending on health averages 0.8 percent of GDP).

A recent World Bank study of the DRC highlights the heavy debt financing of nonviable development projects, especially during the initial period of Mobutu's rule, in 1967-74. Most prominent among these white elephants was a project in 1972 to construct the Inga-Shaba power line, financed in part by the US Export-Import Bank. The project was initiated for strategic purposes, but its cost ballooned to $1.5 billion and its objective

---

2. This seems conservative indeed, considering other reports that his wealth was as high as $9 billion (*Times* of London, 5 May 1997).

was never realized. It is still the largest single contributor to the DRC's outstanding debt. Other white elephants include a $250 million steel mill in Inga financed by the Italian government and a $100 million World Bank loan in 1975 aimed at increasing the output of cobalt and copper mines (the output of which subsequently fell). The structural adjustment loans made by the World Bank and IMF in 1987 and 1989 also almost surely ended up financing activities that had no development benefits. Note, finally, that estimates of capital flight for the period 1970-96 represent more than 150 percent of the total outstanding debt of the DRC.

Kenya

Kenya has an on-again, off-again record of economic reform during the past two decades—characterized by numerous plans and promises made in conjunction with, and with the support of, international donors—that have been either partially or unsatisfactorily enacted. The country has been victim to pervasive corruption, lack of commitment to reform by the political elite, and a number of economic and other shocks that have handicapped it. In the late 1970s, Kenya became the laboratory for what has now come to be known as structural adjustment, and it was the first country to receive the new type of large loans from the IMF and World Bank meant to support stabilization and structural adjustment programs.

The World Bank and IMF struggled with Kenya, unsatisfied with the pace and commitment to the adjustment program, and ended up with a checkered pattern of support during the next two decades, first committing resources and then delaying disbursement and on occasion cutting off Kenya completely. They released resources to support Kenya's reform effort beginning in 1980, cut off funding in 1984-85, reinforced a new plan in 1986, cut off funding again from 1991 to 1993, supported a plan in 1993, and then suspended programs again in 1997 (table C.3). The country experienced impressive growth immediately after independence (1964-70) and moderate growth in the 1970s, but its per capita growth fell to zero in the 1980s and was negative in the 1990s.

Accumulation of Kenyan Debt

From its independence in 1964 until 1979, under the administration of President Jomo Kenyatta, Kenya followed an economic strategy based on strong state control and import substitution, though with a more market-oriented bias than many of its neighbors. It achieved impressive growth during this period (annual GDP growth of more than 5 percent during 1964-80), and was supported consistently by nearly all donors, as well as receiving private financing on commercial terms.

Table C.3 Resource flows and other indicators for Kenya, 1970-99
(millions of constant 1995 dollars, annual averages)

Flow or indicator	1970-79	1980-84	1985-89	1990-94	1995-99	Total, 1980-99
Debt outstanding	2,195	3,319	5,080	6,264	5,846	5,572 (average)
Public and publicly guaranteed	1,600	2,783	4,395	5,505	5,521	5,354
Nonguaranteed	596	536	685	759	326	219
Disbursements	622	754	851	633	376	13,068
PPG disbursements	349	527	632	529	369	10,279
Bilateral	129	156	193	154	127	3,152
Multilateral	100	198	227	224	157	4,034
Private	120	172	212	150	85	3,093
Total debt service	283	509	599	646	648	12,015
PPG debt service	124	356	475	542	556	9,644
Debt transfers	339	245	251	−14	−272	1,054
Grants	211	347	515	751	379	9,959
Total net transfers	549	592	766	737	107	11,012
Debt to GNP	31	42	58	89	60	n.a.
Debt to exports	105	153	236	256	202	n.a.
Debt service to GNP	4	6	7	9	7	n.a.
Export credits						
Capital flight (percentage of GDP)[a]	−0.3	−1.3	3.7	−2.8	−3.9	−0.8
Military spending[b]		246 (1981-84)	266	210	199	4,601 (1980-99)
Arms imports			72	33	26 (1995-97)	
Freedom House ranking	Partly free	Partly free	Not free	Not free	Not free	..
Corruption ranking	..	3	3	3	..	..

n.a. = not applicable

PPG = public or publicly guaranteed

a. Capital flight is measured as Schneider's (2001) estimates for resident capital outflows, adjusted for debt forgiveness and cross-currency valuation for 1990-98. Capital flight data are available from 1975 to 1998. A positive sign represents capital outflow.

b. Swedish International Peace Research Institute, 1998 dollars.

Source: World Bank Global Development Finance CD-ROM, 2001, unless otherwise noted.

In the 1970s, Kenya received $5.5 billion in net transfers, about 70 percent of which came from bilateral sources in the form of concessional loans and grants. Annual net transfers grew consistently, from slightly more than $200 million in 1970 to $1 billion in 1979. During this period, most of the bilateral and multilateral support to Kenya was provided for small discrete projects, and a large share (58 percent) of bilateral assistance was in the form of technical assistance. The result of this external borrowing was the accumulation of a large stock of outstanding debt, but because Kenya managed to grow despite the continuing weaknesses in its economic model, its debt situation was manageable. In 1979, Kenya's $3.3 billion stock of outstanding debt represented only 129 percent of exports, below even the enhanced HIPC Initiative's threshold of 150 percent.

In the late 1970s, a series of shocks—first commodity price declines in coffee and tea and then the second oil shock in 1979—destabilized and exposed underlying inefficiencies in Kenya's economy. When Kenyatta died in 1979, his vice president, Daniel Toroitich arap Moi, took over the presidency, and within a short period set out plans for a complete overhaul of the economy. Kenya received massive amounts of aid in the 1980s conditioned on structural reforms. Bilateral donors increasingly switched their assistance to grants, and the multilaterals moved away from project-based lending in favor of large balance of payments support programs. Between 1980 and 1990, Kenya received more than $8 billion in net transfers, $1.4 billion of which was balance of payments support from the IMF and World Bank.[3]

Despite the increased assistance, Kenya's economy faltered in the 1980s. In the early 1980s, Kenya attempted to comply with stringent IMF fiscal targets to stem inflation, but endemic corruption impeded more structural reforms and Kenya's 3.6 GDP growth rate during the period 1980-85 failed to keep pace with population growth (3.7 percent a year). Kenya experienced a brief recovery in the period 1986-89, but fell into a deep recession again in 1990.

Meanwhile, debt ballooned, topping $6 billion by 1990, now 253 percent of exports. In 1980 Kenya's debt was split relatively evenly between bilateral, multilateral, and private creditors. By 1985, multilaterals held 50 percent of its outstanding debt. This trend was hastened by bilateral debt relief initiatives in the second half of the 1990s that amounted to $700 million. The country was able to avoid arrears on its debt in the second half of the 1980s, due partially to the high levels of balance of payments support it was receiving. The recession in 1990, combined with the removal of balance of payments support in 1991, forced it into arrears that grew quickly, to 15 percent of outstanding debt in 1993.

Kenya's debt peaked in 1995, and it has been falling at about 7 percent annually since (due to bilateral debt forgiveness; multilateral debt has continued to grow). The country's debt has been reduced via the application of traditional Paris Club mechanisms, but it will not receive relief on its nearly $3 billion outstanding debt to the multilaterals, which is below the HIPC threshold and is considered sustainable. In 1999, the IMF

---

3. The major provider of assistance, the United Kingdom, backed away, and was replaced by Japan and the United States. Japan's share of aid to Kenya doubled from 4 to 8.6 percent from the 1970s to 1980s (and doubled again to 17 percent during the period 1990-96).

and World Bank pledged new loans of $300 million to Kenya, contingent on a strict implementation list of anticorruption measures and other conditionalities that Kenya has yet to meet. In 2000, the IMF released $50 million in drought relief to Kenya through its PRGF facility, but has held firm on releasing additional resources. Meanwhile there have been vocal calls from the Kenyan opposition for the international community not to support the Moi regime.

Odious Nature of Kenyan Debt

The argument for odious debt in the Kenyan case is strong. A corrupt ruling elite has expropriated billions of dollars in waste and in amassing personal fortunes. Kenyatta and his family built up a huge fortune in land, precious gems, ivory, and casinos during the 1964-79 period of relatively successful growth and benign economic policy. In 1991, Moi's personal fortune was estimated at $3 billion,[4] and more recently at $4-5 billion. This sum represents 75-85 percent of Kenya's $5.6 billion in publicly guaranteed debt stock and 150 percent of the debt accumulated during Moi's tenure as president. Transparency International's *Global Corruption Report 2001* ranks Kenya as one of the 10 most corrupt countries in the world, and estimates that the Kenyan government lost more than $6 billion through corruption during the period 1991-97 (Transparency International 2001). In 1996, the top 10 percent of Kenya's population earned 47 percent of national income, making it one of the two or three most unequal countries in the world (World Bank 1996).

In 2000, a report of the Kenyan Parliamentary Anti-Corruption Select Committee (known as the Kombo Report) produced a 'list of shame,' which read like a who's who of President Moi's government, and recommended that all on the list be barred from ever holding public office. Among those cited were the vice president, George Saitoti; the minister of tourism, commerce, and industry, Nicolas Biwott;[5] and Moi's son, Gideon Moi.

The ruling elite has had only limited accountability to the Kenyan populace during the past two decades. Soon after taking power in 1964, Kenyatta consolidated power in the Kenyan central authority and instituted a quasi-democratic single-party state. After an unsuccessful coup attempt in 1982, Moi tightened controls on political and civil liberties, and he passed a constitutional amendment solidifying the single-party state. In 1988, the constitution was modified to give the president power to remove public servants and members of the judiciary, and secret ballots were replaced by a system of queue voting. In the same year, Freedom

---

4. *New York Times*, 21 October 1991, A9.

5. Biwott allegedly accumulated hundreds of millions of dollars in overseas accounts, "possibly more than the president himself" (*Los Angeles Times*, 16 November 1991, A16).

House downgraded Kenya's status from partly free to not free, the lowest possible ranking.

In 1991—in response to increased internal resistance and a post-Cold War donor community demanding stricter compliance with democratic and corruption benchmarks—Moi's party rolled back the 1988 amendments. In December 1992, Kenya held its first multiparty elections. Despite this change, Kenya under Moi is still judged not free, democratic, or accountable by most internationally recognized measures.

Among other scandals that could be classified as white elephants are the Goldenberg scam in 1991, when a false exporter of gold and diamonds was paid $400 million in export incentive credits from the government (a deal allegedly authorized by Moi and Saitoti to help finance the 1992 election);[6] Moi's purchase of 12 Mirage fighters from France for $37 million in exchange for a free presidential jet after being offered similar hardware for half the price from the British government (but without a bribe to sweeten the deal);[7] the resale of food aid from Saudi Arabia to the Kenyan government at inflated prices by traders acting for Moi (it was reported that the windfall from one such deal was worth $16 million);[8] and a $25 million soybean processing plant pushed by Asitoti and Biwott against multiple expert opinions that the project was not viable (Kombo Report 2000).

Capital flight was extremely pronounced in the period 1985-87. In the span of 3 years, about $2 billion flowed out of the country, representing 9 percent of annual GDP. However, figures for the 1990s suggest significant repatriation into the country.

Nicaragua

During the past three decades, Nicaragua has been a magnet for politically motivated international financial assistance (table C.4). Periods of oppressive dictatorship and civil war, along with declining terms of trade and other economic shocks, have meant that any benefits of international assistance have not been reaped—while debt has ballooned. Nicaragua's GDP per capita in 1999 was half of what it was in 1975 (in constant 1995 dollars).

Accumulation of Nicaraguan Debt

After an earthquake devastated the city of Managua in 1972, West Point graduate Anastasio Somoza changed the Nicaraguan constitution to allow

---

6. *Time International*, 22 June 1998, 16.

7. *Financial Times*, 27 November 1991, 4.

8. *New York Times*, 21 October 1991, A9.

Table C.4 Resource flows and other indicators for Nicaragua, 1970-99 (millions of 1995 constant dollars, annual averages)

Flow or indicator	1970-79	1980-84	1985-89	1990-94	1995-99	Total, 1980-99
Debt outstanding	1,140	3,447	7,480	9,667	6,032	5,766 (average)
Disbursements	265	417	723	342	327	11,691
Bilateral	51	301	686	201	60	6,751
Multilateral	64	99	22	136	258	3,216
Private	150	16	15	6	10	1,734
Debt service	130	142	37	197	223	4,293
Debt transfers	135	274	686	146	105	7,398
Grants	27	85	164	505	490	6,494
Total net transfers	162	359	850	650	595	13,893
Debt to GNP	38	111	364	1,657	350	n.a.
Debt to exports	134	558	2,017	2,342	699	n.a.
Debt service to GNP	4	5	1	16	13	n.a.
Capital flight (percentage of GDP)	2.4 (1977-79)	− 2.5	22.4	0.5	− 1.7	4.6 (1995-98)
Military spending (percent of GDP)[a]	n.a.	7.1	26 (40-50 percent in 1987)	n.a.	n.a.	n.a.
Arms imports	n.a.	n.a.	612	36	n.a.	n.a.
Freedom House ranking	Partly free	Partly free	Partly free	Partly free	Partly free	(Free in 1998)
Corruption ranking (0-6)	n.a.	3	5	5	n.a.	n.a.

n.a. = not available

a. Swedish International Peace Research Institute Yearbook, various years.

Source: World Bank Global Development Finance CD-ROM, 2001, unless otherwise noted.

for his return to the presidency in 1974, amid increased tension and resistance from the Sandinista National Liberation Front (FSLN) and the Democratic Liberation Union (UDEL). Between 1974 and July 1979, the economic downturn and internal political turmoil in Nicaragua dried up some of the private investment that had been available in the 1960s and early 1970s. But the international community committed $800 million to Nicaragua and disbursed nearly the same amount on new and existing loans. These commitments came primarily from bilateral (US) and multilateral sources.

International assistance financed a growing share of the deficit, as volatility in agricultural commodity prices hurt Nicaragua's exports. The Somoza regime spent much of the assistance on agriculture and infrastructure projects. Domestic resources were thus freed for less legitimate purposes as an export-oriented economic agenda backed by the United States gave Somoza the leverage to engage in corruption and political oppression. He amassed a huge personal fortune during this period. In the 1970s, his family owned 23 percent of land in Nicaragua, and the majority of contracts made on foreign loans were given to his inner circle. His personal wealth is estimated to have reached $500 million in the late 1970s,[9] roughly half the size of Nicaragua's entire debt and 33 percent of its GDP in 1979.

Somoza's agro-export model began to crumble in the second half of the 1970s, as demand for Nicaraguan exports fell and civil infighting increased.[10] In the later 1970s, there was significant capital flight from the country (Ministerio de Cooperación Externa 1991).

The 45-year Somoza family dynasty was toppled on 17 July 1979 by the Sandinistas and replaced by the National Junta of Reconstruction controlled by the leaders of the FSLN. On assuming power, the Sandinistas inherited a $1.6 billion debt accumulated by the Somoza regime. About half the debt was owed to private creditors, and one-quarter each to bilateral and multilateral donors. Nearly 3 years of brutal civil war, coupled with falling commodity prices on international markets and a political regime unconcerned with its citizens' welfare, had left Nicaragua's economy in ruins. In the last 3 years of the Somoza regime, GDP per capita had fallen from $1,069 to $680 (1995 dollars). In 1979, Nicaragua's debt-GDP ratio was 80 percent.

---

9. See http://members.tripod.com/PR0J3CT/somoza.htm.

10. Francisco Laínez, founder of Nicaragua's Central Bank, and known as Nicaragua's economic czar at the end of the Somoza regime, described the use of aid flows during this period as follows: "After the earthquake [that hit Managua in 1972], a lot of money flowed into the country for reconstruction. Until 1976 or 1977, the aid was flowing and there were business deals and reconstruction. When Somoza saw that this aid flow was dwindling down to the last piece of this cake, he said, 'This last piece is mine.' But the monied interests around him said, 'No'" (*Multinational Monitor*, September 1996, vol. 17, no. 9).

The foreign countries responded in 1979. Commitments from official creditors in 1979 jumped to $226 million (up from $64 million in 1978). A large part of this increase was in grants from bilateral donors, which rose from $8.5 million in 1978 to $63 million in 1979; 88 percent of the overall increase came from bilateral donors (Canada and Western Europe), and most of the rest from the Soviet Union. During the next decade, foreign countries continued to pour resources into Nicaragua. Disbursements averaged more than $500 million annually, peaking at $883 million in 1986. Between 1979 and 1990, the international community transferred nearly $6 billion in loans and grants to Nicaragua. These figures are roughly consistent with the increase in the size of Nicaragua's external debt and its balance of payments deficit during this period.

The Sandinistas wasted no time in rescheduling the stock of outstanding debt inherited from the Somoza regime, to allow them space in which to institute their reconstruction and development programs. In December 1980, Nicaragua restructured $582 million (70 percent) of its debt owed to private banks, and reached bilateral debt restructuring agreements with some donors (notably Spain and West Germany), but not with the United States. As the economic situation worsened, Nicaragua continued rounds of rescheduling with private banks, reaching tentative agreements in 1984 and 1985.

In 1985, Nicaragua reached a critical agreement with the Soviet Union and other socialist countries to suspend debt-service payments until 1987. Beginning in 1983, the Sandinista government adopted a policy that debt-service payments would not take precedence over domestic economic and social programs, and it went into arrears with a number of creditors. Bilateral loans were repaid as long as new loans were forthcoming; where they were not, Nicaragua suspended payment. In March 1985, Nicaragua became the first country ever to fall 6 months behind in repaying loans to the World Bank. At that point, Nicaragua's total debt to the World Bank was $134 million.

The composition of flows to Nicaragua changed dramatically in the 1980s. The United States—because of its political opposition to the Sandinista government's relations with the Soviet Union and Cuba—began to cut off economic aid to Nicaragua in 1980. The United States also pressured the multilateral institutions to transfer fewer resources to Nicaragua.[11] The

---

11. Loans that received positive technical evaluations in both the World Bank and the Inter-American Development Bank (IDB) were opposed and eventually terminated by the United States. There are numerous examples of loans between 1982 and 1985 in the IDB that were supported by all members except the United States. An IDB loan in August 1983 ($628,000 for a furniture makers' cooperative in Managua) passed despite US opposition, but it was the last assistance to Nicaragua during the period. Multilateral sources less susceptible to US influence (UNICEF, United Nations Development Program, World Food Program) continued and expanded programs in Nicaragua during this period.

World Bank and Inter-American Development Bank completely ceased lending to Nicaragua in 1984, and in 1985 the United States instituted a trade embargo against Nicaragua. US official action, as well as the political instability instigated by US-financed conterrevolutionary forces (Contras), made private financing unavailable to Nicaragua.

The financing gap left by the withdrawals of the United States and of multilateral and private creditors was filled by bilateral contributions from socialist, West European, and other Latin American countries.[12] This shift implied considerably higher transportation costs for Nicaragua, but also reduced the prices for many products, especially agricultural implements. Credits from the Soviet Union and Eastern Europe were generally provided at less concessional terms (4-5 percent interest rates) with shorter grace periods than those from the multilaterals and Western Europe, but the socialist countries were more willing to renegotiate and postpone payments.

As the US-supported Contras intensified their armed opposition to the Sandinista regime, military spending steadily increased in the 1980s. Data on military spending are limited and controversial, because of the intensely political nature of the Contra-Sandinista struggle. According to the World Bank, Nicaragua was spending 17.5 percent of GDP on its military in 1985, in comparison with the Latin American average of 1.7 percent (table C.5). During the most hostile period, military spending is estimated to have reached 40-50 percent. In 1986, 70 percent of the value of Nicaraguan imports was for military arms. Using these figures, total military spending during the Sandinista regime can be estimated at nearly $5 billion, or 55 percent of Nicaragua's outstanding debt in 1989.[13]

Democracy Returns and Inherits Debt

The democratically elected government that took over in 1990 inherited the $9 billion debt that had accumulated during the previous 15 years. In this period, Nicaragua's debt had multiplied ninefold while GDP per capita fell from $998 in 1975 to $444 in 1991 (1995 dollars). Social indicators deteriorated during this period, and in 1990, Nicaragua had the highest level of infant mortality in the Western Hemisphere.

---

12. Mexico and Venezuela provided grants and petroleum credits to Nicaragua from 1979 to 1982, but halted grants of oil in 1982-83 because of a lack of service payments by Nicaragua. This forced an additional reliance on the Soviet Union, which became the largest supplier of oil to Nicaragua, by 1986 providing 80 percent of the country's oil needs on highly concessional terms.

13. Various estimates suggest that between 20 and 35 percent (approximately $3 billion) of the debt accumulated by Nicaragua and other countries in the developing world during this period is attributable to arms imports.

Table C.5 Military and social spending by Nicaragua, 1979-90

Item	1979	1980	1981	1982	1983	1984	1985	1986	1987	1988	1989	1990
Military expenditure (percent of GDP)	3.1	4.4	5	6	10	11	17	18	40-50	30	n.a.	21
Public spending on education, total (percent of GNP, Unesco)	3	3.4	4.6	4.3	5.1	6.4	5.9	6.2	5.4	3.9	3.3	3.4
Debt service paid (percent of GNP)	4.0	4.4	8.0	7.4	3.5	2.4	2.3	1.3	1.1	0.8	1.1	6.5

n.a. = not available

Sources: Education and debt-service data are from World Bank, *Global Development Finance* CD-ROM, 2001; military expenditure data are from Swedish International Peace Research Institute Yearbook, various years.

The United States and the multilateral institutions responded swiftly to the change in government, and by 1991 they had resumed lending and were supporting a massive adjustment and reform package for the country. Foreign exchange and trade were liberalized, and inflation was attacked and brought under control by 1992.

With the domestic transition, the United States and other bilateral creditors began discussing debt relief with Nicaragua, but debt-service payments jumped as the new government began servicing its debt, including paying the arrears that had been unpaid or rescheduled since 1983.[14] The ratio of debt service to exports rose from 2.5 percent in 1990 to 24.5 percent in 1992, and it nearly doubled to 41.5 percent by 1995. Average annual debt service increased from $63.7 million in the 1980s to $208.2 million in the 1990s. An increasing share of international assistance was provided in grant form. Average annual grants increased from $128 to $454 million in the 1990s. New lending and grant-making in the 1990s to Nicaragua have been dominated by the multilateral institutions, and—coupled with simultaneous bilateral debt relief initiatives—have meant that multilaterals now have the largest share of Nicaragua's debt.

Odious Nature of Nicaraguan Debt

Despite some evidence that Somoza was using international assistance for development purposes, the debt incurred before 1979 under the Somoza regime has all the components of odiousness. Somoza was unrepresentative and unaccountable to the Nicaraguan populace, and he used the cover of international assistance to loot his country of hundreds of millions of dollars. His personal fortune and the record of land and other holdings seized by him and his cronies is evidence to this point.

The debt accumulated in the 1980s under the Sandinista regime looks odious on two counts. There was a high level of military spending although some might argue this was forced on the country by the US-financed Contras. Similarly, the data show massive capital flight, although they are particularly uncertain.

Pakistan

Pakistan is a country with a large population of more than 140 million that was thrust into unwanted prominence on the world stage in September 2001 as a result of its proximity to Afghanistan. A small but passionately committed part of its population opposes the side its government

---

14. In September 1991, the United States forgave 80 percent of the debt ($259.5 million) owed to it by Nicaragua.

has taken in the war on terrorism, but the dangers for the cohesion of a state that was already riven by ethnic and religious differences have so far shown no sign of materializing. Indeed, it is conceivable that the cash infusion that results from the conflict will give Pakistan the chance to pull its economy out of the perpetual semi-crisis of the past decade (table C.6).

Accumulation of Pakistani Debt

The country has not always been an economic cripple. Although it had virtually no industry when it was created out of the division of British India in 1947, by the early 1960s it was exporting more manufactures than such East Asian countries as Indonesia, Malaysia, the Philippines, and Thailand. Its agriculture flourished for several decades, based on a rapid expansion of irrigation and enthusiastic adoption of the techniques of the Green Revolution. GNP increased at more than 5 percent a year from the late 1950s to the late 1980s, by far the best performance of any South Asian country. Only social indicators spoiled the picture: literacy was still only 35 percent; infant mortality was still at 111 per thousand; the total fertility rate was 4.6; and above all there was a horrendous gender gap, with the proportion of girls in primary school, for example, as low as 32 percent.[15]

In the 1990s, growth slumped to little more than 4 percent a year, while the rest of South Asia saw an acceleration, so that Pakistan became the region's slowest-growing rather than fastest-growing economy. Pakistan was forever going to the IMF and signing programs that it failed to complete (a record that was finally broken in 2001).

What went wrong? First, the tragic aftermath of the wars with India was a long-term diversion of public expenditure from the social sectors to the military, a deflection that undermined the prospects for social advance and curtailed the human capital formation necessary for rapid growth.

Second, the government of Zulfikar Ali Bhutto, which took office in 1972, pursued a set of policies that in retrospect appear utterly perverse: widespread nationalization (one of the last countries to engage in this before privatization replaced it on the reform agenda), dissolution of the "elitist" civil service of Pakistan, and restoration of the power of large landlords. Third, the military dictatorship of Zia ul Haq, which seized power in 1977, failed to reverse the misguided economic policies of his predecessor while magnifying corruption and accentuating the emphasis on the military.

Fourth, the ethnic and religious fissures that had plagued Pakistan after its creation were aggravated by the 1980s war against the Soviet

---

15. These are 1990 figures (World Bank, *World Development Indicators* CD-ROM, 2000).

Table C.6 Resource flows and other indicators for Pakistan, 1970-99 (millions of constant 1995 dollars, annual averages)

Flow or indicator	1970-79	1980-84	1985-89	1990-94	1995-99	Total, 1980-99
Debt outstanding	11,976	11,701	15,393	21,050	27,117	30,561
Public and publicly guaranteed	11,942	11,665	15,313	20,286	24,988	28,351
Nonguaranteed	34	36	80	764	2,129	2,208
Disbursements	1,847	1,873	1,764	2,991	3,375	68,486
PPG disbursements	1,632	1,417	1,581	2,483	2,510	56,271
Bilateral	1,173	648	616	811	954	26,874
Multilateral	275	356	767	1,317	1,162	20,759
Private	184	413	198	356	394	8,644
Debt service	626	963	1,389	2,177	2,653	42,178
PPG debt service	617	947	1,358	1,988	2,114	38,210
Debt transfers	1,220	910	375	814	722	26,308
Grants	275	572	681	620	320	13,723
Total net transfers	1,496	1,482	1,057	1,434	1,042	40,031
Debt to GNP	43	30	35	40	44	n.a.
Debt to exports	348	163	190	210	244	n.a.
Debt service to GNP	2	2	3	4	4	n.a.
Capital flight (percent of GDP)	0.3 (1976-79)	-0.3	2.3	0.2	-0.9 (1995-97)	
Military spending		2,216	3,125	3,452	3,499 (1995-97)	
Arms imports			584	909	610 (1995-97)	
Freedom House ranking	Partly free	Not free	Partly free	Partly free	Partly free	(Not free from 1999-)
Corruption ranking (0-6)	..	1	2	2	..	..

n.a. = not applicable

PPG = public or publicly guaranteed

Sources: World Bank *Global Development Finance* CD-ROM, 2001; Military expenditure data are from Swedish International Peace Research Institute *Yearbook,* various years.

occupation of neighboring Afghanistan. Fifth, the democratic governments that succeeded the military dictatorship of 1977-88 were dominated by an intense personal rivalry between Benazir Bhutto and Nawaz Sharif, both of whom were more intent on enlarging their family fortunes than serving the social good, and neither of whom was prepared to risk short-term political popularity for long-term national gain.

Odious Nature of Pakistani Debt

One criterion for identifying debts as odious is if the government that contracts them is a dictatorship rather than one that commands the consent of the governed. Pakistan was ruled by a military dictator, Zia ul Haq, from 1977 to 1988. He sought to legitimize his hold on power through a referendum in 1984 and elections for the National and Provincial Assemblies in 1985, which gave him some modicum of democratic legitimacy, although that was quickly compromised by a constitutional amendment designed to concentrate power in his hands that was introduced by decree. His hold on power was ended only when he and a number of military colleagues were killed in an air crash believed to have been caused by espionage in 1988.

Democracy was restored in the following months. There then followed a decade of alternating power between Benazir Bhutto and Nawaz Sharif, each of whom won two elections and served terms of something more than 2 years each time, before being dismissed by the president (and in the last case replaced by a military coup) on the grounds of chronic corruption. In 1999, Pakistan reverted to a military dictatorship in the person of General, now President, Pervez Musharraf (who so far has a reputation for benevolence and has promised to restore democracy in due course).

This history might make one uneasy about applying the criterion of democratic rule to judge whether debts should be judged as odious or legitimate. Would one rule that all debts incurred by Zia ul Haq were odious, or would those incurred after he acquired his veneer of democratic legality be deemed legitimate? Would the debts incurred under the highly corrupt but democratically elected governments of Bhutto and Sharif be deemed legitimate? Should Musharraf have been denied access to international loans, a decision that would inevitably have prompted a moratorium on debt service, meaning mainly servicing of loans contracted by the Bhutto and Sharif governments? Could this conceivably have made Pakistan better off, meaning that the country would have been rewarded for having installed a dictator? Or should his government be denied access to new loans if and when it reneges on its promise to restore democracy? What would an expectation that it might be denied access to new loans in the future do to its current ability to borrow, and thus maintain the service of old loans? These are uncomfortable questions, to which there are no obvious answers.

A second criterion for debts to be judged odious might be that they were incurred to buy armaments. Pakistan has indeed been a heavy purchaser of armaments, as the data in table C.6 show. Were such debts automatically judged odious, the country would presumably have been unable to buy those arms, which its government (and probably most of its population) judged necessary to maintain a convincing defensive capability against India. Should the international community then decide on the legitimacy of a country's decisions to purchase arms? Could the international community then stand aside if a country whose desire to buy arms for self-defense was denied were subsequently to be attacked? This criterion also appears fraught with problems when its implications are examined carefully.

A third criterion for odious debts might be if they were used to finance capital flight. The statistics reveal net capital flight from Pakistan during the period 1976-97, but the total amount is rather insignificant. There appears to have been more capital flight in the late 1980s, but little or no flight in the 1990s, presumably because expatriate Pakistanis sent back more money than was spirited out by resident Pakistanis. That does not mean that capital flight has not been a problem in Pakistan; both the Bhutto and Sharif families are known to have accumulated substantial foreign wealth. In macroeconomic terms, however, this is not a big factor. Could one sensibly declare all the country's foreign debts to be odious because a small part of them had been used to build up the foreign wealth of its rulers?

The fourth and final criterion for debt to be considered odious is that it be used to finance white elephants. Pakistan has undoubtedly had its share of white elephants. Indeed, a recent report to the Pakistani government (Debt Reduction and Management Committee 2001, 21) identified three important programs as falling into this category: a program for building motorways (expressways to Americans), investment in Saindak copper, and the Tamir-i-Watan program (which gave public money to every member of Parliament to spend on good works in his constituency; i.e., enabled him to buy votes). The total expenditure on these three programs in the 1990s amounted to about 172 billion rupees, 28 percent of 1995 GDP, suggesting that wasteful investments may have approached 3 percent of GDP in a typical year. This is quite substantial, although it does not explain the bulk of the capital inflows or foreign debt. In sum, all the characteristics that make people judge debt to be odious were indeed present to some degree in Pakistan.

Uganda

Uganda has been the most successful country in the HIPC context, reaching its completion point under both the original and enhanced initiatives for a total of $2 billion in debt-stock relief (table C.7). In the 1990s, Uganda was a model reformer, with considerable commitment to an economic reform program that produced impressive growth. Uganda has also undertaken a process of national consultations and dialogue resulting in a homegrown national poverty reduction strategy that has provided the framework for all other HIPCs struggling to implement the PRSP process.

Accumulation of Ugandan Debt

Uganda's success in the 1990s came in the context of a highly unsustainable debt situation. Its debt as a percentage of exports peaked in 1992 at 1,223 percent. Since then, this ratio has been declining due to strong export growth. Uganda amassed its $3 billion outstanding debt during the preceding two decades, although mainly in the 1980s. Under the 1971-79 regime of Idi Amin, external assistance from the international community was limited. Although initially supportive of the transfer of power from Milton Obote to Amin in 1971, bilateral and multilateral donors became worried by Amin's tactics and military spending, and most suspended support in 1972. Nonetheless, the Amin administration did receive some bilateral support from Russia and Arab states related to Cold War alignments. Uganda's outstanding debt was slightly more than $500 million in 1971, and it was about $800 million when Amin fled the country in 1979.

The expulsion of Amin in 1979 and the elections in 1980 (the first in 18 years) were taken as positive signals by the international community. Beginning in 1980, Uganda received massive amounts of external assistance. Unlike most other African countries, most of this assistance to Uganda came from multilateral donors, primarily the IMF and World Bank. The international community supported the Obote regime between 1981 and 1984, and it endorsed the policies for inflation control and fiscal austerity designed jointly with the IMF.

The economy that had been devastated by Amin in the 1970s made a short comeback in the early 1980s. The IMF agreed to three standby arrangements and disbursed about $600 million in balance of payments support to Uganda between 1980 and 1984. The World Bank reengaged with Uganda as well, disbursing $200 million in IDA financing during this period. Overall, creditors disbursed $2 billion between 1980 and 1986, and Uganda's outstanding debt more than doubled from $600 million to $1.4 billion (282 percent of exports).

During this period, Uganda fell into an increasingly violent civil conflict, and the government spent upward of 30 percent of revenues on the military. The Obote government's 4-year military effort resulted in greater loss of life than Amin's 8-year rule (an estimated 500,000 were killed during the period 1980-85). Yet unlike Amin, Obote was very sensitive about his international image, and realized the importance of securing

Table C.7 Resource flows and other indicators for Uganda, 1970-99 (millions of constant 1995 dollars, annual averages)

Flow or indicator	1970-79	1980-84	1985-89	1990-94	1995-99	Total, 1980-99
Debt outstanding	523	717	1,657	2,611	3,301	3,544
Disbursements	91	127	297	299	218	4,702
Bilateral	32	22	78	61	17	893
Multilateral	15	61	147	223	200	3,156
Private	43	45	72	14	0	656
Debt service	31	58	90	111	102	1,806
Debt transfers	60	69	207	188	115	2,895
Grants	54	129	211	432	491	6,316
Total net transfers	113	198	418	620	606	9,211
Interest arrears	5	14	39	89	56	64
Principal arrears	19	53	94	252	214	226
Debt to GNP	0	36	28	73	54	
Debt to exports	69	160	398	1,028	448	
Debt service to GNP	0	3	2	3	2	
Capital flight (percentage of GDP)		2.7	2.2	−0.2	−2.1 (1995-98)	
Freedom House ranking	Not free	Partly free	Partly free	Not free	Partly free	
Corruption ranking (0-6)	..	1	3	3	..	

Source: World Bank Global Development Finance CD-ROM, 2001.

external assistance for both economic recovery and continued financing of his war effort. He followed IMF conditionalities even when they were politically costly (e.g., devaluing the currency and postponing plans to reinstitute one-party rule).

The intense civil conflict showed signs of resolution in 1986, after Obote fled the country. In response, the World Bank and IMF stepped up their policy-based lending to Uganda. Bilateral donors followed suit. Total net transfers jumped to about $500 million in 1987 and have stayed there consistently to the present. Uganda's debt ballooned in this period, doubling again by 1993. About half of assistance to Uganda in the 1980s was loans associated with structural adjustment programs, and a large share of bilateral loans and grants was for technical assistance. The economic recovery program instituted in 1987 was slow to show results but eventually succeeded, bringing growth in exports and GDP back to Uganda. Since the beginning of the 1990s, aid coordination has improved in Uganda, the government has shown strong commitment to the reform program, and Uganda has used technical assistance uncharacteristically well.[16]

Odious Nature of Uganda's Debt

External assistance to Uganda from 1986 to the present has been one of the central factors allowing Uganda's economic recovery. Critics may take issue with the amounts disbursed, but the support that Uganda received from multilateral and bilateral sources seems to have been used for development purposes, and relatively effectively, during this period.

Before 1986, however, it is reasonable to assume that little of the money given to Uganda was used effectively for development purposes. This includes the large share of lending, mostly by the multilaterals, to the second Obote regime between 1980 and 1985. The Obote regime was unaccountable to its citizens and singularly focused on using military means to quiet its critics and adversaries. Capital flight during this period was 2.7 percent of GDP. The high levels of military spending and growing intensity of the internal civil conflict may well have signaled to the creditor community that this was an environment where resources were not going to be used well. And in 1985, when Obote fled the country, he allegedly took much of the nation's wealth with him. Uganda's $1.4 billion outstanding debt in 1986 represented almost half of its total HIPC-eligible debt.

Loans given to Uganda under Amin fall even more clearly into the odious category. After all, his regime seems to fit all the criteria: not accountable to the public, expropriating money for its own purposes and checking accounts, and using money to finance non-development-related

---

16. See Holmgren, Dollar, and Shanta (1999).

expenditure. But as has been explained, lending to Uganda during this period was limited, and in 1980 enough of the Amin debts were forgiven to allow Uganda's debt to fall back to its pre-1971 levels.

The case of Uganda in 1980 presents a quandary for the practical application of an odious debt doctrine. Perhaps forgiving Uganda's entire $800 million debt in 1980 would have been consistent with the decision by the IMF and the international community as a whole to reengage in Uganda. With the benefit of hindsight, this would only have freed up even more resources for the high military spending and non-development-focused Obote regime in the early 1980s, a regime whose debts we might now declare odious as well. The massive infusion of international assistance, mainly multilateral, beginning in 1986 could have been accompanied by some debt reduction based on an odious debt doctrine, but that would have been a gamble considering the fragile political situation and lingering internal conflict.

References

Addison, Tony, and Aminur Rahman. 2001. Resolving the HIPC Problem: Is Good Policy Enough? Paper presented at a World Institute for Development Economics Research conference on debt, Helsinki (August).

Birdsall, Nancy, Stijn Claessens, and Isaac Diwan. 2001. *Will HIPC Matter? The Debt Game and Donor Behavior.* Carnegie Endowment for International Peace Economic Reform Project Discussion Paper 3. Washington: Carnegie Endowment for International Peace.

Birdsall, Nancy, and Amar Hamoudi. 2002. *It's Not about Trade Policy! Commodity Dependence, Trade, Growth, and Poverty.* Center for Global Development Working Paper 3. Washington: Center for Global Development.

Boone, Peter. 1996. Politics and the Effectiveness of Foreign Aid. *European Economic Review* 40: 289-329.

Booth, David. 2001. PRSP Processes in Eight African Countries: Initial Impacts and Potential for Institutionalization. Paper presented at a World Institute for Development Economics Research conference on debt, Helsinki (August).

Boyce, James, and Leonce Ndikumana. 2001. Is Africa a Net Creditor? New Estimates of Capital Flight from Severely Indebted Sub-Saharan African Countries, 1970-96. Paper presented at a World Institute for Development Economics Research conference on debt, Helsinki (August).

Burnside, Craig, and David Dollar. 2000. Aid, Policies, and Growth. *American Economic Review* 90, no. 4 (September).

Burnside, Craig, and Domenico Fanizza. 2001. Hiccups for HIPCs. Paper presented at a World Institute for Development Economics Research conference on debt, Helsinki (August).

Carnegie Endowment for International Peace. 2001. *The Role of the Multilateral Development Banks in Emerging Market Economies.* Washington: Carnegie Endowment, EMP Financial Advisers, and Inter-American Dialogue. http://www.ceip.org/econ (April 2001).

Chinnock, Jeffrey. 1998. In Whose Benefit: The Case for Untying Aid. ActionAid Policy Briefing (April).

Cohen, Daniel. 2000. *The HIPC Initiative: True and False Promises.* Organization for Economic Cooperation and Development Working Paper. Paris: OECD Development Centre.

Collier, Paul. 2000. Consensus Building, Knowledge, and Conditionality. Paper presented at the annual World Bank conference on development economics, Washington (April 18-20).

Collier, Paul, and David Dollar. 2000. Can the World Cut Poverty in Half? Washington: World Bank. (Forthcoming in *World Development*.)

Culpeper, Roy, and John Serieux. 2001. *Journeys Just Begun: From Debt Relief to Poverty Reduction*. Ottawa: North-South Institute.

Debt Reduction and Management Committee. 2001. *A Debt Burden Reduction and Management Strategy*. Islamabad: Finance Division, Government of Pakistan.

Devarajan, Shantayanan, Vinaya Swaroop, and Heng-fu Zou. 1996. The Composition of Public Expenditure and Economic Growth. *Journal of Monetary Economics* 37: 313-44.

Dijkstra, Geske, and Niels Hermes. 2001. The Uncertainty of Debt Service Payments and Economic Growth of HIPCs: Is There a Case for Debt Relief? Paper presented at a World Institute for Development Economics Research conference on debt, Helsinki (August).

Drop the Debt. 2001. *Reality Check: The Need for Deeper Debt Cancellation and the Fight Against HIV/AIDS*. Washington: Drop the Debt.

Easterly, William. 1999. *How Did Highly Indebted Poor Countries Become Highly Indebted? Reviewing Two Decades of Debt Relief*. Washington: World Bank.

Easterly, William. 2001. *The Elusive Quest for Growth*. Cambridge, MA: MIT Press.

Eichengreen, Barry, and Peter H. Lindert. 1989. *The International Debt Crisis in Historical Perspective*. Cambridge, MA: MIT Press.

Einhorn, Jessica. 2001. The World Bank's Mission Creep. *Foreign Affairs* 80, no. 5 (September/October): 22-35.

Ellerman, David. 2001. *Helping People Help Themselves: Toward a Theory of Autonomy-Compatible Help*. World Bank Operations Evaluation Department Working Paper no. 7 (June). Washington: World Bank.

Eurodad (European Network on Debt and Development). 2000. *Rethinking HIPC Debt Sustainability*. http://www.eurodad.org (July).

Eurodad (European Network on Debt and Development). 2001. *Putting Poverty Reduction First*. http://www.eurodad.org (October).

Freedom House. 2001. *Freedom in the World: Annual Rankings of Political and Economic Freedom*. http://www.freedomhouse.org/ratings/index.htm (October).

GAO (US General Accounting Office). 2000. *Debt Relief Initiative for Poor Countries Faces Challenges*. Washington: US General Accounting Office.

Hansen, H., and Finn Tarp. 2001. Aid and Growth Regressions. *Journal of Development Economics* 64: 547-70.

Kanbur, Ravi. 2001. Economic Policy, Distribution and Poverty: The Nature of Disagreements. *World Development* 29, no. 6: 1083-94.

Kanbur, Ravi, and Todd Sandler. 1999. *The Future of Development Assistance: Common Pools and International Public Goods*. Overseas Development Council Policy Essay 5. Washington: Overseas Development Council.

Holmgren, Torgny, Dollar, David, and Devarajan Shanta. 1999. Uganda. In *Aid and Reform in Africa: Lessons from Ten Case Studies*. Washington: World Bank.

Kiakwama, Gilbert, and Jerome Chevallier. 2000. Democratic Republic of Congo. In *Aid and Reform in Africa: Lessons from Ten Case Studies*. Washington: World Bank.

Kombo Report *(Report of the Kenyan Parliamentary Anti-Corruption Select Committee)*. 2000. Nairobi: Parliament of Kenya.

Kremer, Michael, and Seema Jayachandran. 2001. Odious Debt. Harvard University, Cambridge, MA. Photocopy (November).

Krugman, Paul. 1988. Financing versus Forgiving a Debt Overhang. *Journal of Development Economics* 29 (November): 253-68.

Lancaster, Carol. 1999. *Aid to Africa: So Much to Do, So Little Done*. Chicago: University of Chicago Press.

Lerrick, Adam. 2000. HIPC: The Initiative Is Lacking. *Euromoney* (September).

Marshall, Alison. 2001. A Campaigner's Perspective on PRSPs. Paper presented at a World Institute for Development Economics Research conference on debt, Helsinki (August).

Martin, Matthew. 1997. A Multilateral Debt Facility: Global and National. In *International and Monetary Issues for the 1990s*, UN Conference on Trade and Development, vol. 8. New York: United Nations Press.

McCarthy, Eugene. 2001. Debt Relief in Africa: Is It Working? A Civil Society View on the Experience of Uganda, Tanzania, and Mozambique. Bread for the World Institute *Debt and Development Dossier* no. 6 (June).

Meltzer Commission (International Financial Institutions Advisory Commission). 2000. *Report to the US Congress*. http://www.house.gov/jec/imf/ifiac.htm.

Mijumbi, Peter J. 2001. Uganda's External Debt and the HIPC Initiative. *Canadian Journal of Development Studies* 21, no. 2: 445-526.

Ministerio de Cooperación Externa. 1991. *Entre la agresión y la cooperación: La economía Nicaragüense y la cooperación externa en el período 1979-89*. Managua, Gobierno de Nicaragua.

O'Brien, F.S., and Terry Ryan. 1999. Kenya. In *Aid and Reform in Africa: Lessons from Ten Case Studies*. Washington: World Bank.

Overseas Development Council. 2000. *The Future Role of the IMF in Development*. Washington: Overseas Development Council.

Oxfam. 2001. *Debt Relief: Still Failing the Poor*. Oxford: Oxfam International.

Pearson, Lester B. 1969. *Partners in Development: Report of the Commission on International Development*. New York: Praeger Publishers.

Pettifor, Ann, Bronwen Thomas, and Michela Telatin. 2001. *HIPC—Flogging a Dead Process*. London: Jubilee Plus.

Political Risk Services. 2000. *International Country Risk Guide*. Syracuse: Political Risk Services.

Raffer, Kunibert. 2001. Debt Relief for Low Income Countries: Arbitration as the Alternative to Present Unsuccessful Debt Strategies. Paper presented at a World Institute for Development Economics Research conference on debt, Helsinki (August).

Ranis, Gustav, and Frances Stewart. 2001. The Debt-Relief Initiative for Poor Countries: Good News for the Poor? Paper presented at a World Institute for Development Economics Research conference on debt, Helsinki (August).

Rodrik, Dani. 2000. Development Strategies for the Next Century. Paper presented at the annual World Bank conference on development economics, Washington, (April 18-20).

Roodman, David. 2001. *Still Waiting for the Jubilee: Pragmatic Solutions for the Third World Debt Crisis*. Washington: Worldwatch Institute.

Sachs, Jeffrey. 1990. A Strategy for Efficient Debt Reductions. *Journal of Economic Perspectives* 4, no. 1 (Winter).

Sachs, Jeffrey, Kwesi Botchway, Maciej Cuchra, and Sara Sievers. 1999. *Implementing Debt Relief for the HIPCs*. Center for International Development Working Paper. Cambridge, MA: Center for International Development.

Schneider, Benu. 2001. *Measuring Capital Flight: Estimates and Interpretations*. London: Overseas Development Institute.

Sen, Amartya. 1999. *Development as Freedom*. New York: Alfred Knopf.

Serieux, John. 2001. The Enhanced HIPC Initiative and Poor Countries: Prospects for a Permanent Exit. *Canadian Journal of Development Studies* 21, no. 2: 527-48.

Serieux, John, and Yiagadeesen Samy. 2001. The Debt Service Burden and Growth: Evidence for Low-Income Countries. Paper presented at a World Institute for Development Economics Research conference on debt, Helsinki (August).

Soros, George. 2001 *Draft Report on Globalization*. New York: PublicAffairs.

Stiglitz, Joseph. 1999. The World Bank at the Millennium. *Economic Journal* 108, no. 459 (November): 577-97.

Thomas, Melissa. 2001. Getting Debt Relief Right. *Foreign Affairs* 80, no. 5 (September/October): 36-45.

Transparency International. 2001. *Global Corruption Report 2001.* http://www.globalcorruptionreport.org (June).

United Nations. 2000. *Report of the High-Level Panel on Financing for Development* (Zedillo Report). http://www.un.org/reports/financing/ (June).

Van de Walle, Nicolas. 2001. *African Economies and the Politics of Permanent Crisis, 1979-99.* Cambridge: Cambridge University Press.

Were, Maureen. 2001. The Impact of External Debt on Economic Growth and Private Investment in Kenya: An Empirical Assessment. Paper presented at a World Institute for Development Economics Research conference on debt, Helsinki (August).

WHO Commission (World Health Organization Commission on Macroeconomics and Health). 2001. *Macroeconomics and Health: Investing in Health for Economic Development.* Final Report of the Commission. Geneva: World Health Organization.

Winkler, Max. 1933. *Foreign Bonds: An Autopsy.* Philadelphia: Roland Swain.

World Bank. 1996. *World Development Report 1996: From Plan to Market.* New York: Oxford University Press.

World Bank. 1998. *Assessing Aid: What Works, What Doesn't, and Why.* Washington: World Bank.

World Bank. 2000a. *Can Africa Claim the 21st Century?* Washington: World Bank.

World Bank. 2000b. *World Development Report 2000/2001.* New York: Oxford University Press.

World Bank. 2001a. Financial Impact of the HIPC Initiative: First 23 Country Cases. http://www.worldbank.org/hipc (August).

World Bank. 2001b. *Global Development Finance 2001.* Washington: World Bank.

World Bank and IMF. 2001a. The Challenge of Maintaining Long-Term Debt Sustainability. http://www.imf.org/external/np/hipc/2001/lt/042001.htm (April).

World Bank and IMF. 2001b. Enhanced HIPC Initiative—Completion Point Considerations. Washington. Photocopy (17 August).

Wurzel, Eckhard. 2001. *The Economic Integration of Germany's New Länder.* OECD Economics Department Working Paper 307. Paris: Organization for Economic Cooperation and Development.

Glossary

Additionality. Whether, and the extent to which, new forms of resource transfers to developing countries (debt relief being one) are additional to the existing resources provided.

Arrears. Payments due but not paid, on a cumulative basis.

Debt service due. The interest and principal owed by a country to its creditors in a given year.

Debt stock. The total value of the principal owed by a country.

Debt transfers. Loans minus debt service.

Defensive lending. New loans made to allow the borrower to repay older loans falling due and to prevent default. Also known as "forced" lending (see chapters 2 and 5).

EU. European Union.

Eurodad *(European Network on Debt and Development).* Association of European NGOs that has been active in research and advocacy on debt issues (see chapters 2 and 5).

GDP *(gross domestic product).* The total value of all the goods and services produced within a nation.

GNP *(gross national product).* The total value of all the goods and services produced by a nation's residents.

Gross transfers. The sum of loans and grants provided to a country.

G-7 *(Group of Seven).* An organization of seven major industrial nations (Canada, France, Germany, Italy, Japan, United Kingdom, and United States) that meets to discuss international economic issues. When a reference is to the "G-8," Russia is also included.

HIPC *(heavily indebted poor country).* See box 1.1.

IBRD *(International Bank for Reconstruction and Development).* The traditional "hard-window" lending agency of the World Bank that lends to middle-income developing countries at rates commensurate with the bank's cost of borrowing.

IDA *(International Development Association).* The "soft-window" lending agency of the World Bank that makes highly subsidized concessional loans to low-income developing countries.

IMF. International Monetary Fund.

MDBs *(multilateral development banks).* The World Bank, regional development banks, and subregional development banks (appendix A lists the MDBs participating in the HIPC Initiative).

MDGs. Millennium Development Goals.

Net transfers. Gross transfers minus debt service.

NPV *(net present value).* The value of debt, equal to the sum of all future debt-service obligations (interest and principal) on existing debt, discounted at the market interest rate. Because much of the debt of HIPCs was contracted on concessional (below-market) interest rates, NPV is a more appropriate measure of the burden that a country's debt stock imposes.

ODA *(official development assistance).* Loans or grants provided to developing countries on concessional terms (if a loan, having a grant element of at least 25 percent). ODA must have the promotion of economic development and welfare as its main objective; loans and grants for military purposes are excluded.

Odious debt. Debt incurred without the consent of the people and not for their benefit (see chapter 4 and appendix C).

OECD *(Organization for Economic Cooperation and Development).* A group of 30 industrial countries.

OECD DAC *(Development Assistance Committee).* The principal body through which the OECD deals with issues related to cooperation with developing countries (see box 4.1).

OPEC *(Organization of Petroleum Exporting Countries).* A group of countries that seeks to coordinate petroleum production and pricing policies.

Paris Club. An ad hoc group of official creditor countries that coordinates the restructuring of bilateral debt (see footnote 4, chapter 2).

PNG *(private, nonguaranteed)* **debt.** Debt that is an obligation of a private debtor and is not guaranteed for repayment by a public entity.

PPG *(public or publicly guaranteed)* **debt.** Public debt is mostly that of national governments; publicly guaranteed debt is mostly that of state enterprises.

Preferred creditor. A creditor that a borrowing government is obligated to pay back before other creditors. The MDBs and the IMF are preferred creditors, which gives them more security of repayment.

PRGF *(Poverty Reduction and Growth Facility).* The IMF's medium-term lending facility for low-income countries (formerly the Enhanced Structural Adjustment Facility, or ESAF).

Program support. Loans and grants to finance a government's general budget, and not earmarked for specific projects. Also known as program-based aid.

Project support. Loans and grants to finance specific projects in developing countries. Also known as project-based aid.

PRSP *(Poverty Reduction Strategy Paper).* See box 6.1.

RDBs. Regional development banks.

SDR *(Special Drawing Right).* A synthetic currency created by the IMF in 1969 that serves as the IMF's unit of account for transactions and operations. The SDR's value is based on a basket of currencies, and is currently valued at approximately 1 SDR = $1.25.

Selectivity. Provision of resources to developing countries according to a clear set of performance benchmarks, as opposed to strategically motivated or defensive lending (see chapters 4 and 6).

Tied aid. Aid given under the condition that some or all is used to purchase goods and/or services from providers based in the donor country (see chapter 4).

Index

accountability
  creditor, and failure of development assistance, 34-35
  donor, incremental proposals to increase, 108-09
  IMF *versus* World Bank, 108*n*, 108-09
  for project-based aid, 73*n*, 73-74
accounting, aid, 55, 56*b*, 108
additionality, 3, 55-61, 116
  of bilateral loans, 58-59
  and debt relief, 79
  definition of, 50
  under enhanced HIPC Initiative, 58
Afghanistan, 141
African countries. *See* sub-Saharan Africa; *specific country*
African Development Bank (AfDB), 15, 59, 69
aid
  fungibility of, 69, 73, 116
  project-based (*See* project-based aid)
  tied (*See* tied aid)
aid accounting, 55, 56*b*, 108
aid architecture, 101-14, 118
  reinvention of, 6-7
aid coordination, 6, 64*b*, 67, 67*f*, 68
aid efficiency, 3, 50, 63, 64*b*, 66-75
  definition of, 66-75
  and failure of development assistance, 34, 35

and ownership, 66-68
and private investment, 72-75, 116
and project-based aid, 69-71, 70*t*
and reduced transaction costs, 68-69, 116
and selectivity, 76, 78, 110-13
and tied aid, 71-72
aid fatigue, political issues of, 50-51
aid programs. *See also* development assistance
  versus debt relief, 3-4, 10, 49-78, 113, 116-17
  needed to achieve Millennium Development Goals, 46-47
  by sector, 67, 67*f*
Alliance of Democratic Forces for the Liberation of Congo (ADFLC), 127
Amin, Idi, 143, 145-46
amortization payments, reduction in, 65, 65*n*
Angola, 28, 81*n*, 84*n*
arbitration proceedings, 114
Argentina, 13*n*
arms expenditures, 52, 54, 73
  Nicaragua, 136, 136*n*, 137*t*, 138
  Pakistan, 142
  Uganda, 145
Asian Development Bank (ADB), 99*n*
Azerbaijan, 89

country performance, assessment of, 110,
111*b*-112*b*, 113
Country Policy and Institutional
Assessment (CPIA) index, 76, 110,
112*b*
credit counseling, independent, 109
creditor accountability, and failure of
development assistance, 34-35
creditworthiness constraint, 73
Cuba, 52
currency depreciation, 14*b*, 91

DAC. *See* Development Assistance
Committee (DAC)
debt
amount of, 8
bilateral (*See* bilateral loans)
breakdown by creditor, 24*f*
burden of, measures of, 28, 32
commercial, value of, 8
net transfers on, 17, 48
odious (*See* odious debt)
public, 89
rescheduling of, 5
uncollectible, amount of, 8
debt campaign, 115
central players in, 11
political momentum behind, 51-52
debt contracts, sanctity of, 49, 73
debt-export ratios, 21
as criterion for debt relief calculation,
38, 42, 80, 89, 90*t*
under enhanced HIPC Initiative, 28,
30*t*-31*t*, 32, 36, 42-44, 44*f*, 80
of heavily indebted poor countries, 21
lower case sensitivity analysis, 43, 44*f*
projected, 42-44, 44*f*
debt-GDP ratios, 21
under enhanced HIPC Initiative, 28,
30*t*-31*t*, 32
of heavily indebted poor countries, 19,
21
debt relief. *See also* HIPC Initiative; loans,
writing off
accounting standards for, 55, 56*b*, 108
additional, financing of, 4-5, 93-100, 95*f*
versus aid programs, 3-4, 10, 49-78, 113,
116-17
cost to donors, 37-38, 93, 95, 95*f*
efficiency advantage of, 74-75, 79
expansion of, 4-6, 79-100, 116-17, 117
full
arguments against, 79-80

versus partial, 10, 47-48, 63-64, 74,
79-80
merits of, 2
official, first efforts at, 22, 23*b*
political arguments for, 54
transfer-neutral, 68-69, 78
who should pay for, 9
debt-service ratios, 19, 20*f*, 80-81
post-HIPC Initiative, 32
debt servicing
burden of, 5-6, 80-81
measures of, 32
diversion of funds from social
expenditures to, 36-38, 79, 80-81,
105
Eurodad formula for, 84, 85*t*, 86, 86*n*,
95, 95*f*
2 percent GNP threshold for, 81, 82*t*-
83*t*, 84, 89, 90*t*, 95, 95*f*
Oxfam formula for, 80-81, 82*t*-83*t*, 84
and project-based aid, 70-71
relief from, 5, 25
generated by enhanced HIPC
Initiative, 47-48, 79
trust funds for, 25, 76
debt stock cancellation, 22, 23*b*, 25-26, 81
debt sustainability, 25
analysis of
at completion point, 39-40
World Bank-IMF, 38-40, 39*f*, 43, 43*n*
countries projected to reach, without
HIPC assistance, 81*n*, 84*n*
under enhanced HIPC Initiative, 41-44,
80-100
decision point
consolidation of completion point and,
105-06
debt-service ratios at, 81, 82*t*
debt sustainability analysis at, 40
definition of, 26, 102
under enhanced HIPC Initiative, 27*n*,
27-28, 28*t*, 30*t*-31*t*
and PRSP development, 104-05
and selectivity ratings, 112*b*
defaulting, sovereign, history of, 13, 14*b*-
15*b*
Democratic Liberation Union (UDEL),
134
Democratic Republic of Congo, 54, 124-
28, 125*t*
development, steps critical to, 11
development assistance. *See* aid
programs; official development
assistance (ODA)

Development Assistance Committee
(DAC), 41, 55, 56b, 71n, 72, 108, 109
development strategy, control of. *See*
ownership
dictatorships, 141
disincentive effect, 81
distributional effects. *See also*
redistribution
of debt cancellation, 49, 65-66, 86
definition of, 50
Dollar, David, 50, 63, 64b, 66, 75
domestic reforms, needed to achieve
development goals, 46, 47b, 101
donor accountability, incremental
proposals to increase, 108-09, 118
donor conduct, principles for, 6, 109-10,
118
donor confidence
and private investment, 72-75
and selectivity, 75-76, 78
donors. *See also specific institution*
case for more from, 41-48
coordination of, 6, 64b, 67, 67f, 68, 109
and cost of debt relief, 37-38, 93, 95,
95f, 99
and recipients
contract between, 113-14
distinction between, 99
"down the rathole" argument, for failure
of development assistance, 33, 35
drinking water, safe, access to, 45, 47b
Drop the Debt, 1, 27n, 37, 51, 58, 63

earthquakes, Managua, 132, 134n
Eastern Europe, 99n, 136
economic governance
and failure of development assistance,
33, 35-36, 64b, 73-74
prudent, penalties for, 89, 89n
rating of, 111b-112b
education
gender equality in, 45, 47b
primary, universal, 45, 47b
eligibility
expansion of, 4, 86-91, 95, 95f
HIPC Initiative standards, 26n, 26-32,
36-38
political pressure and, 37
enclave extractive sectors, 15n
enhanced HIPC Initiative, 2b, 23b, 26-32,
115-16
additionality, 58
completion point under, 27-28, 29t, 36
conditionality under, 35-36

cost of, 4, 59, 60b, 65-66, 79, 81, 82t-83t,
95, 95f
countries eligible under, 28, 29t
critiques of, 33-40
debt-export ratio under, 28, 30t-31t, 32,
36, 42-44, 44f, 80
debt relief standards under, 42
debt-service relief generated by, 47-48
debt sustainability under, 41-44, 80-100
decision point under, 27n, 27-28, 28t,
30t-31t
design of, and new aid architecture,
102-06
eligibility standards, 26n, 26-32, 36-38
expansion of, 117
cost of, 89, 90t, 99, 117-18
net present value (NPV) under, 30t-
31t, 32, 36, 42-44, 44f
poverty reduction under, 27, 41
rationale for, 3
technical issues, 36
Enhanced Structural Adjustment Facility,
17. *See also* Poverty Reduction and
Growth Facility (PRGF)
equity effect, 81
Eritrea, 88
Ethiopia, 28
Eurodad (European Network on Debt
and Development), 11, 80
debt servicing formula, 84, 85t, 86, 86n,
95, 95f
HIPC eligibility criterion suggested by,
36-38
European Union
bilateral debt reduction, 84n
conversion of loans to grants by, 22,
22f
official development assistance from,
evolution of, 22, 22f
evergreening, 5
export credits, 15, 35
cancellation of, accounting standards
for, 56b, 108
export growth rates, 39f, 39-40, 43, 92.
See also debt-export ratios
export price shocks. *See* shocks

fiat reserve asset, 96n
finance ministry types. *See* Group A
("finance ministry types")
financial integrity, of multilateral
institutions, effect of debt
cancellation on, 37, 58, 63

Indonesia, 63, 66, 88
 inclusion in expanded initiative, costs
  of, 91, 95, 97-100, 99*n*, 117-18
 odious debt in, 52-53
infant mortality, 10, 45, 47*b*, 136
Inter-American Development Bank (IDB),
  59, 135*n*, 136
interest arrears, accounting standards
  for, 56*b*, 108
interest rates, lower, 5
International Bank for Reconstruction
  and Development (IBRD), 17, 98
International Country Risk Guide, 123
International Development Association
  (IDA), 7
 conversion of loans to grants by, 106-
  07, 107*n*
 Debt Reduction Facility, 23*b*
 "Fifth Dimension," 76*n*
 fund cancellation, effects of, 63, 65
 loan disbursements to low-income
  countries, 16-17, 17*f*
International Monetary Fund (IMF), 15
 approach of, *versus* World Bank, 108*n*,
  108-09
 contingency facility, 93, 98-100, 117
 cost of HIPC Initiative for, 59
 debt initiatives, 23*b*, 25-26
 debt owed to, breakdown by country
  classification, 24, 24*f*
 debt sustainability analyses, 38-40, 39*f*,
  43, 43*n*
 financial integrity of, effect of debt
  cancellation on, 37, 58, 63
 financing of additional relief by, 4
 future role in development, 62*b*
 gold reserves, mobilization of, 59*n*, 59-
  61, 63, 66, 95-96, 98, 100, 117
 Letters of Intent to, 102
 transfer of PRGF facility from, 7, 61,
  62*b*, 108-09, 118
investment
 foreign direct, 46
 private
  aid efficiency and, 72-75, 116
  and donnor confidence, 72-75, 80
 public, and project-based aid, 70-71

Japan, and HIPC Initiative, 28
Jubilee movement, 1, 11, 26, 27, 27*n*, 115
 biblical foundation of, 51
Jubilee Plus, 1

Kaunda, Kenneth, 108
Kenya, 54, 81*n*, 128-32, 129*t*
Kenyan Parliamentary Anti-Corruption
  Select Committee, 131
Kenyatta, Jomo, 128, 131
Keynes, John Maynard, 14*b*
Kombo Report, 131
Krueger, Anne, 114*n*
Kyrgyzstan, 88, 89

Laínez, Francisco, 134*n*
Lao PDR, 28
Latin America. *See also specific nation*
 debt restructuring, 15*b*
 loan defaults, 14*b*
leadership
 and corruption, 131, 134, 138, 141, 145
 and failure of development assistance,
  35
lending
 discipline in, 6, 109-10, 118
 efficiency of, and failure of
  development assistance, 34, 35-36
 forced, 76, 78
 sovereign, history of, 13, 14*b*-15*b*, 21
loans
 bilateral (*See* bilateral loans)
 conversion to grants, 5, 43, 76, 78, 97,
  106-08
  by European Union, 22, 22*f*
 evergreening of, 5
 multilateral (*See* multilateral loans)
 to purchase G-7 goods, 9
 writing off, 5-6 (*See also* debt relief;
  HIPC Initiative)
  history of, 14*b*
  partially *versus* completely, 10, 47-48,
   63-64, 74, 79-80
London terms (Paris Club), 23*b*
lower case sensitivity analysis, debt-
  export ratio, 43, 44*f*
lower-middle-income countries, list of,
  122
low-income countries
 aid statistics, 57, 57*f*
 classification scheme, 15*n*
 debt statistics, 87-89, 88*t*
  by creditor, 24*f*
  multilateral loans, 16-17, 17*f*
 expansion of HIPC Initiative to, cost
  of, 89, 90*t*, 99, 117
 list of, 121
Lyons terms (Paris Club), 23*b*

Other Publications from the Institute for International Economics

* = out of print

POLICY ANALYSES IN INTERNATIONAL ECONOMICS Series

1 The Lending Policies of the International Monetary Fund*   John Williamson
   August 1982   ISBN 0-88132-000-5
2 "Reciprocity": A New Approach to World Trade Policy?*   William R. Cline
   September 1982   ISBN 0-88132-001-3
3 Trade Policy in the 1980s*
   C. Fred Bergsten and William R. Cline
   November 1982   ISBN 0-88132-002-1
4 International Debt and the Stability of the World Economy*   William R. Cline
   September 1983   ISBN 0-88132-010-2
5 The Exchange Rate System*, Second Edition
   John Williamson
   Sept. 1983, rev. June 1985 ISBN 0-88132-034-X
6 Economic Sanctions in Support of Foreign Policy Goals*
   Gary Clyde Hufbauer and Jeffrey J. Schott
   October 1983   ISBN 0-88132-014-5
7 A New SDR Allocation?*   John Williamson
   March 1984   ISBN 0-88132-028-5
8 An International Standard for Monetary Stabilization*   Ronald L. McKinnon
   March 1984   ISBN 0-88132-018-8
9 The YEN/Dollar Agreement: Liberalizing Japanese Capital Markets* Jeffrey A. Frankel
   December 1984   ISBN 0-88132-035-8
10 Bank Lending to Developing Countries: The Policy Alternatives*   C. Fred Bergsten, William R. Cline, and John Williamson
   April 1985   ISBN 0-88132-032-3
11 Trading for Growth: The Next Round of Trade Negotiations*
   Gary Clyde Hufbauer and Jeffrey R. Schott
   September 1985   ISBN 0-88132-033-1
12 Financial Intermediation Beyond the Debt Crisis*   Donald R. Lessard, John Williamson
   September 1985   ISBN 0-88132-021-8
13 The United States-Japan Economic Problem*
   C. Fred Bergsten and William R. Cline
   October 1985, 2d ed. January 1987
                              ISBN 0-88132-060-9
14 Deficits and the Dollar: The World Economy at Risk*   Stephen Marris
   December 1985, 2d ed. November 1987
                              ISBN 0-88132-067-6

15 Trade Policy for Troubled Industries*
   Gary Clyde Hufbauer and Howard R. Rosen
   March 1986   ISBN 0-88132-020-X
16 The United States and Canada: The Quest for Free Trade*   Paul Wonnacott, with an Appendix by John Williamson
   March 1987   ISBN 0-88132-056-0
17 Adjusting to Success: Balance of Payments Policy in the East Asian NICs*
   Bela Balassa and John Williamson
   June 1987, rev. April 1990 ISBN 0-88132-101-X
18 Mobilizing Bank Lending to Debtor Countries*   William R. Cline
   June 1987   ISBN 0-88132-062-5
19 Auction Quotas and United States Trade Policy*   C. Fred Bergsten, Kimberly Ann Elliott, Jeffrey J. Schott, and Wendy E. Takacs
   September 1987   ISBN 0-88132-050-1
20 Agriculture and the GATT: Rewriting the Rules*   Dale E. Hathaway
   September 1987   ISBN 0-88132-052-8
21 Anti-Protection: Changing Forces in United States Trade Politics*
   I. M. Destler and John S. Odell
   September 1987   ISBN 0-88132-043-9
22 Targets and Indicators: A Blueprint for the International Coordination of Economic Policy*   John Williamson and Marcus H. Miller
   September 1987   ISBN 0-88132-051-X
23 Capital Flight: The Problem and Policy Responses*   Donald R. Lessard and John Williamson
   December 1987   ISBN 0-88132-059-5
24 United States-Canada Free Trade: An Evaluation of the Agreement*
   Jeffrey J. Schott
   April 1988   ISBN 0-88132-072-2
25 Voluntary Approaches to Debt Relief*
   John Williamson
   Sept.1988, rev. May 1989 ISBN 0-88132-098-6
26 American Trade Adjustment: The Global Impact*   William R. Cline
   March 1989   ISBN 0-88132-095-1
27 More Free Trade Areas?*
   Jeffrey J. Schott
   May 1989   ISBN 0-88132-085-4
28 The Progress of Policy Reform in Latin America*   John Williamson
   January 1990   ISBN 0-88132-100-1
29 The Global Trade Negotiations: What Can Be Achieved?*   Jeffrey J. Schott
   September 1990   ISBN 0-88132-137-0
30 Economic Policy Coordination: Requiem or Prologue?*   Wendy Dobson
   April 1991   ISBN 0-88132-102-8

Pacific Dynamism and the International Economic System*
C. Fred Bergsten and Marcus Noland, editors
May 1993   ISBN 0-88132-196-6

Economic Consequences of Soviet Disintegration*
John Williamson, editor
May 1993   ISBN 0-88132-190-7

Reconcilable Differences? United States-Japan Economic Conflict*
C. Fred Bergsten and Marcus Noland
June 1993   ISBN 0-88132-129-X

Does Foreign Exchange Intervention Work?
Kathryn M. Dominguez and Jeffrey A. Frankel
September 1993   ISBN 0-88132-104-4

Sizing Up U.S. Export Disincentives*
J. David Richardson
September 1993   ISBN 0-88132-107-9

NAFTA: An Assessment
Gary Clyde Hufbauer and Jeffrey J. Schott/rev. ed.
October 1993   ISBN 0-88132-199-0

Adjusting to Volatile Energy Prices
Philip K. Verleger, Jr.
November 1993   ISBN 0-88132-069-2

The Political Economy of Policy Reform
John Williamson, editor
January 1994   ISBN 0-88132-195-8

Measuring the Costs of Protection in the United States
Gary Clyde Hufbauer and Kimberly Ann Elliott
January 1994   ISBN 0-88132-108-7

The Dynamics of Korean Economic Development*
Cho Soon
March 1994   ISBN 0-88132-162-1

Reviving the European Union*
C. Randall Henning, Eduard Hochreiter, and Gary Clyde Hufbauer, editors
April 1994   ISBN 0-88132-208-3

China in the World Economy   Nicholas R. Lardy
April 1994   ISBN 0-88132-200-8

Greening the GATT: Trade, Environment, and the Future   Daniel C. Esty
July 1994   ISBN 0-88132-205-9

Western Hemisphere Economic Integration*
Gary Clyde Hufbauer and Jeffrey J. Schott
July 1994   ISBN 0-88132-159-1

Currencies and Politics in the United States, Germany, and Japan
C. Randall Henning
September 1994   ISBN 0-88132-127-3

Estimating Equilibrium Exchange Rates
John Williamson, editor
September 1994   ISBN 0-88132-076-5

Managing the World Economy: Fifty Years After Bretton Woods   Peter B. Kenen, editor
September 1994   ISBN 0-88132-212-1

Reciprocity and Retaliation in U.S. Trade Policy
Thomas O. Bayard and Kimberly Ann Elliott
September 1994   ISBN 0-88132-084-6

The Uruguay Round: An Assessment*
Jeffrey J. Schott, assisted by Johanna W. Buurman
November 1994   ISBN 0-88132-206-7

Measuring the Costs of Protection in Japan*
Yoko Sazanami, Shujiro Urata, and Hiroki Kawai
January 1995   ISBN 0-88132-211-3

Foreign Direct Investment in the United States, 3rd Ed.   Edward M. Graham and Paul R. Krugman
January 1995   ISBN 0-88132-204-0

The Political Economy of Korea-United States Cooperation*
C. Fred Bergsten and Il SaKong, editors
February 1995   ISBN 0-88132-213-X

International Debt Reexamined*   William R. Cline
February 1995   ISBN 0-88132-083-8

American Trade Politics, 3rd Ed.   I.M. Destler
April 1995   ISBN 0-88132-215-6

Managing Official Export Credits: The Quest for a Global Regime*   John E. Ray
July 1995   ISBN 0-88132-207-5

Asia Pacific Fusion: Japan's Role in APEC*
Yoichi Funabashi
October 1995   ISBN 0-88132-224-5

Korea-United States Cooperation in the New World Order*
C. Fred Bergsten and Il SaKong, editors
February 1996   ISBN 0-88132-226-1

Why Exports Really Matter! *   ISBN 0-88132-221-0
Why Exports Matter More!*   ISBN 0-88132-229-6
J. David Richardson and Karin Rindal
July 1995; February 1996

Global Corporations and National Governments
Edward M. Graham
May 1996   ISBN 0-88132-111-7

Global Economic Leadership and the Group of Seven   C. Fred Bergsten and C. Randall Henning
May 1996   ISBN 0-88132-218-0

The Trading System After the Uruguay Round*
John Whalley and Colleen Hamilton
July 1996   ISBN 0-88132-131-1

Private Capital Flows to Emerging Markets After the Mexican Crisis*   Guillermo A. Calvo, Morris Goldstein, and Eduard Hochreiter
September 1996   ISBN 0-88132-232-6

The Crawling Band as an Exchange Rate Regime: Lessons from Chile, Colombia, and Israel
John Williamson
September 1996   ISBN 0-88132-231-8

Flying High: Liberalizing Civil Aviation in the Asia Pacific*
Gary Clyde Hufbauer and Christopher Findlay
November 1996   ISBN 0-88132-227-X

Measuring the Costs of Visible Protection in Korea*   Namdoo Kim
November 1996   ISBN 0-88132-236-9

The World Trading System: Challenges Ahead
Jeffrey J. Schott
December 1996   ISBN 0-88132-235-0

DISTRIBUTORS OUTSIDE THE UNITED STATES

Australia, New Zealand, and
Papua New Guinea
D.A. Information Services
648 Whitehorse Road
Mitcham, Victoria 3132, Australia
tel: 61-3-9210-7777
fax: 61-3-9210-7788
e-mail: service@dadirect.com.au
http://www.dadirect.com.au

United Kingdom and Europe
(including Russia and Turkey)
The Eurospan Group
3 Henrietta Street, Covent Garden
London WC2E 8LU England
tel: 44-20-7240-0856
fax: 44-20-7379-0609
http://www.eurospan.co.uk

Japan and the Republic of Korea
United Publishers Services, Ltd.
Kenkyu-Sha Bldg.
9, Kanda Surugadai 2-Chome
Chiyoda-Ku, Tokyo 101
Japan
tel: 81-3-3291-4541
fax: 81-3-3292-8610
e-mail: saito@ups.co.jp
For trade accounts only.
Individuals will find IIE books in
leading Tokyo bookstores.

Thailand
Asia Books
5 Sukhumvit Rd. Soi 61
Bangkok 10110 Thailand
tel: 662-714-0740-2 Ext: 221, 222, 223
fax: 662-391-2277
e-mail: purchase@asiabooks.co.th
http://www/asiabooksonline.com

Canada
Renouf Bookstore
5369 Canotek Road, Unit 1
Ottawa, Ontario K1J 9J3, Canada
tel: 613-745-2665
fax: 613-745-7660
http://www.renoufbooks.com

India, Bangladesh, Nepal, and Sri Lanka
Viva Books Pvt.
Mr. Vinod Vasishtha
4325/3, Ansari Rd.
Daryaganj, New Delhi-110002
India
tel: 91-11-327-9280
fax: 91-11-326-7224
e-mail: vinod.viva@gndel.globalnet.
ems.vsnl.net.in

Southeast Asia (Brunei, Cambodia,
China, Malaysia, Hong Kong, Indonesia,
Laos, Myanmar, the Philippines, Singapore
Taiwan, and Vietnam)
Hemisphere Publication Services
1 Kallang Pudding Rd. #04-03
Golden Wheel Building
Singapore 349316
tel: 65-741-5166
fax: 65-742-9356

Visit our Web site at:
http://www.iie.com
E-mail orders to:
orders@iie.com